www.Aspatore.com

Aspatore Books is the largest and most exclusive publisher of C-Level executives (CEO, CFO, CTO, CMO, Partner) from the world's most respected companies. Aspatore annually publishes a select group of C-Level executives from the Global 1,000, top 250 professional services firms, law firms (Partners & Chairs), and other leading companies of all sizes. C-Level Business Intelligence ™, as conceptualized and developed by Aspatore Books, provides professionals of all levels with proven business intelligence from industry insiders – direct and unfiltered insight from those who know it best – as opposed to third-party accounts offered by unknown authors and analysts. Aspatore Books is committed to publishing a highly innovative line of business books, and redefining such resources as indispensable tools for all professionals. Aspatore is a privately held company headquartered in Boston, Massachusetts, with employees around the world.

Inside the Minds

The critically acclaimed *Inside the Minds* series provides readers of all levels with proven business intelligence from C-Level executives (CEO, CFO, CTO, CMO, Partner) from the world's most respected companies. Each chapter is comparable to a white paper or essay and is a future-oriented look at where an industry/profession/topic is heading and the most important issues for future success. Each author has been carefully chosen through an exhaustive selection process by the *Inside the Minds* editorial board to write a chapter for this book. *Inside the Minds* was conceived in order to give readers actual insights into the leading minds of business executives worldwide. Because so few books or other publications are actually written by executives in industry, *Inside the Minds* presents an unprecedented look at various industries and professions never before available.

Inside The Minds:
Leading
Deal Makers

Industry Leaders Share Their Knowledge on Negotiations, Leveraging Your Position and the Art of Deal Making

Published by Aspatore Books, Inc.
For information on bulk orders, sponsorship opportunities or any other questions please email store@aspatore.com. For corrections, company/title updates, comments or any other inquiries please email info@aspatore.com.

First Printing, 2002
10 9 8 7 6 5 4 3 2 1

ISBN 1-58762-058-8

Library of Congress Card Number: 2001119971

Cover design by Michael Lepera/Ariosto Graphics & Kara Yates

Material in this book is for educational purposes only. This book is sold with the understanding that neither any of the authors or the publisher is engaged in rendering legal, accounting, investment, or any other professional service.

This book is printed on acid free paper.

A special thanks to all the individuals that made this book possible.

Special thanks to: Jo Alice Hughes, Rinad Beidas, Kirsten Catanzano, Melissa Conradi, Molly Logan, Justin Hallberg

The views expressed by the individuals in this book do not necessarily reflect the views shared by the companies they are employed by (or the companies mentioned in this book). The companies referenced may not be the same company that the individual works for since the publishing of this book.

If you are a C-Level executive interested in submitting a manuscript to the Aspatore editorial board, please email jason@aspatore.com with the book idea, your biography, and any additional pertinent information.

Inside the Minds:
Leading Deal Makers
Industry Leaders Share Their Knowledge on Negotiations, Leveraging Your Position and the Art of Deal Making

<u>Contents</u>

BRINGING ADDED VALUE TO THE DEAL PROCESS

MARY ANN JORGENSON

Squire, Sanders & Dempsey

Coordinator of Business Practice Area

Adding Value With Personal Style

One of the reasons I enjoy deals more than anything else I do is that there is so much room for adding ideas and finding workable paths through a maze of problems toward desired results. I never start from the idea that what the client says he wants done today is necessarily the best we can do together. A good deal maker does not travel blindly down a prescribed path, but rather is always looking for side-roads to improve the client's prospects.

The way to add value to client situations is by bringing your own ideas into the mix and your own ways to get things done. Clients want that. My clients don't usually say, "OK, Mary Ann, here's what I want you to do. Take steps 1, 2, and 3, stop there, and we'll talk about it again." The relationship is much more personal, much more trusting. I go out to the end of the rope, see what's there, come back, and check in. Then we devise new goals, approaches, and possibilities. So, we do not begin with absolutes and certainties, but rather with possibilities to explore.

Things in my background probably contribute to my comfort with the ambiguities of working this way. First of all, I was an English major, then an English teacher. When you teach poetry, you take a poem apart, and then help your students put it back together again. Deal making is similar to that process: breaking things down into parts, analysis, small epiphanies, and ultimately, problem-solving. It's seeing the mosaic and how the pieces fit together. Having that kind of background has made me very comfortable in a "deal world."

I think being a teacher also made me very comfortable with a roomful of people, all having different ideas and different goals. Granted, sometimes I'm a bit of a schoolmarm in my approach to it. I want control of the situation – I'll admit that. But standing up in front of a group or being responsible for how a meeting goes – all of that is very comfortable for me; I am not bothered by chaos. As a result, it's a pleasure to be in situations with 25 people in the room, with four agendas, but with a deal as the goal. So, from my perspective, people who come into a room with a list of four points they have to win are at a disadvantage. They usually are inflexible and not nimble enough to add real value.

Also, I started in the law business ten years late. I didn't go to law school right out of college. I got a master's degree in teaching at Harvard, taught for five years, and had two kids. So I was ten years out of college when I started as a lawyer. I think that meant I was given more credit than I deserved at the beginning, but I had more real-world experience than most of my colleagues, so I was a little more comfortable that way, too.

And I have always been one who prefers not to know what's coming around the corner. I enjoy coming in each day, not knowing what's going to happen. I revel in not knowing. I have a new challenge, something new to think about and fix or find a way through, so it's always interesting. Nothing becomes routine. It keeps my interest up and my mind prepared.

This is not the same thing as not wanting to anticipate what the other side is going to do. My practice has been split between mergers and acquisitions, on the one hand, and proxy fights, tender offers, and fights for control of companies on the other hand. In the latter group, anticipation is everything. You don't want to be surprised.

You want to try to figure out every move the other side could make and be ready for it.

The Attention Factor

Deal making requires extraordinary attention, both the focused kind that makes certain all the issues are covered in the negotiations, and the documents and the details are accurate, but also the scattered kind of focus that comes from having all your antenna up, noticing body language of the participants, picking up on cues that suggest there is more to a certain comment or fact than has yet been disclosed. At the same time you have to be sure your own body language and comments are not giving away more information than you intend!

The attention factor plays a large role in your perceived value to your client, as well. His trust in you is built on prior experience – your ability to sense when he needs assurance, or an explanation of what impact certain language in a contract may have two years down the road, your ability to sense which issues he would want to decide himself (and no two clients have the same list). Making sure the client is kept as "close" to the deal process as his comfort zone requires, and just as importantly, bringing alternatives to his attention, even when he has not asked you to find them – these behaviors demarcate the really strong deal makers from the merely competent.

Friendly vs. Hostile Deals

In a friendly deal, you'll have tense moments, and three or four potential deal breaker issues. Different companies have different levels of tolerance, for example, for environmental problems. You have to find ways to share the pain of potential environmental liabilities that satisfy both parties. So there is negotiation; there is tension; there are two sides to lots of issues. But both parties want to get to the same goal line, where one wants to sell, and one wants to buy; otherwise, we wouldn't be talking.

In a contested deal, nothing is agreed, including having any conversation at all. If you're being attacked, you don't want the other person in the room. If you're the raider, you want to get enough stock in your hands that you can control the company, whether you do it with a proxy contest or a real offer to buy shares. None of it is friendly or genteel.

When the deal is hostile, I meet with my client, and we go down every road we can think of to a satisfactory result, trying to anticipate what issues will come up. Then I move into a mode of total toughness, even though I am not always conscious of it. I insist on playing by the rules – federal and state securities and corporate laws apply to hostile offers. If the other side goes over the line, I use the rules to try to get them back in line. It's total attention, total focus, and total toughness.

When the deal is friendly, I'm often talking with my client about whether it's worth it to make some new piece of knowledge a big issue: For example, the seller didn't tell us there was a problem at a major manufacturing facility, but we found out about it anyway, during due diligence. Is it really worth making this a big issue, when we're going to need their cooperation on 14 other items? We're going to need them to support us with their employees, so their employees don't leave before we buy the company. We're going to need them to cement customer relationships and help us through the transition in customer relationships. I think the wiser course is to pick your fights; don't go at the other side tooth and nail over every little issue.

In both friendly deals and unfriendly deals that involve price, I think getting the pricing right is the most challenging part for both the businesspeople and the lawyers.

Most people probably think lawyers have very little to do with pricing. That's not true. Some clients don't want or need another voice in the pricing decision. But often when a client becomes worried because he doesn't think he can afford the price the seller is demanding, you can help him see the values of the synergies of the two businesses; you can help him think through what growth means to him and whether it's worth paying a little more to move the company up a notch in his market. It's the closeness to the client, being available as a good sounding board when he comes to those moments of doubt. It's a very intangible thing. Some lawyers do it better than others; some think it's not part of their job, but I've always seen it as one of the most important parts.

Perseverance Pays

The test as to whether a lawyer added value to a deal is not whether the deal closed. Some deals fail because they should. It was a gleam in the buyer's eye, or the seller's eye, before any diligence was done. As the buyer learns more, he may learn things that should tell him this is not the right company, or it's not the right time, or it's not the right price at this time. I don't feel like a failure when that happens. On the contrary, if I was helpful in getting and evaluating information that allows my client to review his options better, I feel like a success. I was part of a successful process of evaluating whether a deal should happen.

Some of my best work – the things I'm proudest of – may be just a very small part of the deal itself. My favorite example occurred during the process of taking a company public. It was a limited partnership, and we were going to take it public as a master limited partnership in the late 1980s. In those days, a limited partnership had to have a general partner with significant net worth. The typical pattern was to have a managing general partner, owned by management with very little net worth. Then a group of other, outside individuals, who personally had significant net worth, would form a special general partner. By agreeing to become a general partner, they would be paid a huge fee, which was really like "renting" their net worth. The limited partnership needed it, and there were wealthy people around who were willing to accept some exposure for a fee.

In this deal, the CEO, who was near retirement, was being made chairman, and another officer would become CEO before the offering. A group of partners from a Texas law firm represented one of the underwriters who wanted to form an entity to serve as the special general partner. I sat down with the underwriters and said, "No. The chairman, who has built this company almost from scratch, ought to be the special general partner and get the $1 or $2 million a year payment. It will look much better in the offering document, and the buyers of the stock will appreciate this expression of the chairman's faith in the company. These Texas guys have no relationship with the company."

It took ten days. I was in New York with a tax lawyer on my side and all these other lawyers on the other side. Every day, I would come in and say, "So, the chairman's going to be the special general partner, right?" And they would come up with a new excuse for why that wouldn't work. By the end of each day, I thought I had it back on track, and I'd come in the next morning, and they'd give me more excuses. But ten days later, I finally got it, and I was on top of the world. I had created something nobody expected, and all the other parties to the transaction finally accepted it. Everyone in the client's family was happy. But it would not have happened if I had just sat there and let things go by.

Teamwork Invaluable for Success

Deal making is a very personal thing – you bring your own personality and your own way of handling people and handling issues to the table. That's part of it. The other part of it is your firm's ability to provide very high-quality support: excellent associates, excellent tax input, top-notch anti-trust talent – and now my firm is providing all of this globally.

The last deal I did involved facilities in 19 countries. We had anti-trust lawyers in Brussels doing the European Union part and anti-trust lawyers in Washington; they all had to work together. We had filings in Spain, in the Czech Republic, Germany, Portugal – we had to have seamless teamwork, with talent and resources. You can't be a successful deal maker by yourself.

Making deals is different with different specialties. On the tax side, where my firm has extraordinary talent, someone often says, "You can't do it this way." They know my next request will be to find a way to do what the client needs. Eventually, they get there. They find a way to do what we want to do. They bring a value that, in a way, can't be compensated.

On the anti-trust side, when you get right down to the core, the talent lies in being able to define the markets in which the companies are operating broadly enough so that if these two companies combine, they don't have a big percentage of the particular market. You don't have an anti-trust problem if you have a lot of competitors left after the proposed transaction. If Company A's purchase of Company C means they'll have 40 percent of the market, you're starting up a very long hill. If the market is seen as big enough that when you combine the two, they have only 10 percent, that's a winner. You need the kind of talent who can think creatively about markets, keep talking to the businesspeople to learn enough about the products to be able to spark some creativity in the businesspeople, to spark another definition, another viewpoint, another vision, of what the market is and also be able to convince the regulators that their definition is correct. Often, businesspeople are paid to show they have a huge share of the market for their products. We're asking them to think bigger, differently, so the market is something else, where the combined business will have only a small share. This is quite a challenge, and the people who do it well are very, very valuable.

Cool Counts

If my client and the other side are both public companies, which is usually the case, I'll begin preparing by reading everything that has been filed with the SEC (Securities and Exchange Commission) within the last five years. If I see a list of material contracts in the Form 10K exhibits, I'll get those exhibits, and I'll read those contracts. The hype about the "persona" you bring into the room is a small percentage of the equation; the other part is total preparation. I've never seen really good lawyers "wing it" through negotiations. They're prepared.

Preparation time depends on how big the deal is. For example, the last one I was talking about was a billion-Euro deal. There were too many contracts for me to read, but not enough for me to have any true idea of what the real risks of the business were.

This deal was an auction. In an auction situation, there's a data room, where the seller puts documents so each bidder has access to those documents. If there are a hundred contracts, you have to rely on your team to have read them and found problem areas and summarized them for you. I'll read the memo, then, rather than read all the contracts.

When negotiations begin, I ask a lot of questions, so I can feel as though I have a real sense of the issues. The client team will talk about what we want to accomplish today, in this meeting – the issues on our agenda to deal with today.

During negotiations, I try very hard to avoid pounding the table, yelling, walking out of the room, any kind of dramatics – whether with great bravado or not. I avoid temper tantrums, planned or not. I try to avoid saying, "That's a deal breaker."

I'll try to postpone an issue I can't resolve, once I see that I can't resolve it, or I realize that my counterpart on the other side of the table has no authority to resolve it, that I need more input from the businesspeople, or that we need to go at this in a different way. When that happens, I'll say, "I don't think we're going to get any further with this today. Let's just table it and think about it overnight."

I don't decide by myself when it's time to give in to the other side or let a point go. I'll take a break and talk with the CEO, or if he's not there, whoever is responsible for the negotiations. We'll go out of the room and talk. I'll tell him what I think, and he'll tell me what he thinks, and if he thinks we can still go further, I'll try everything I can think of to go further.

There does come a time when you give on an issue, or at least you table it till you find out what the other issues are that you can't agree on. And then you start horse trading.

The worst thing that can happen during negotiations is a loss of trust. Every situation is different, but if there's a fact or situation the other side didn't tell you, then, naturally, you start thinking about what else is out there. Why didn't they tell us? Do they think we're so dumb we wouldn't find out? What else are they hiding? The atmosphere can deteriorate dramatically – or not – depending on how the side that has the problem deals with it. How up-front are they once we find out? What is their excuse for not having told us about the problem?

A sense of humor helps. I have a lot more fun when everybody is relaxed.

Dealing With Deal Risk

I think deal risk is highest when you're a buyer who's going to sign and close the same day. You are essentially at risk until the very end. Anything can happen. The seller is at risk, too. Anyone can change his mind if you don't sign a contract until the day you're planning to close the deal. That's the most risky. That's where I worry the most.

The least risky for the buyer is the big deal that's been publicly announced and has no financing conditions, few or no anti-trust issues, and a break-up fee, such that if the buyer decides he isn't going to go through with it, he pays you $20 million (or other significant amount), and you both agree that's the limit of the damages. Another source of break-up fee arises when the seller feels he has to have some kind of market check, some way to accept a higher offer if it comes in on the theory that he owes it to his shareholders to be able to accept a higher bid, and he is willing to pay the buyer the break-up fee in case he does accept a higher bid. The buyer is still disappointed, but at least he has recouped his expenses and some value of his own time and his staff's time.

Invaluable Advice

One of my partners once said to me, "Mary Ann, there are at least 15 ways to say, 'Screw you.' You don't have to be totally direct all the time." I've tried to take that to heart because I'm a very direct person.

When I'm giving advice to our youngest people, the second- and third-year associates, I find myself saying, "You need to be aware of some of the politics here." There are politics in every deal, intra-buyer and intra-seller politics. A lot of decoding of even what your client is saying depends on the context – the political context, or sometimes it's merely the business context: Has the business been doing well? Who has access to what information? Don't just go blithely around asking the client's people questions. You don't even know who knows about this deal. You have to be very careful where you step.

When I'm working with an older associate – sixth- or seventh-year associates – they are really handling the diligence, the documents, and a lot of the details. They'll come to me when they want advice about how to resolve an issue, or how to get beyond this particular failure. We talk about it, and I give them what I think is just totally common-sense advice. Or I'll call the client and get through the barrier because that's what I'm for. But so much of the advice I give is common sense and practical thinking-it-through. The golden rules of deal making apply here: Get prepared. Be practical. Stay contained and calm.

You Can't Be a Wimp

To become a leader in making deals, lawyers have to have shown either senior partners in the law firm who have worked with them or a client who will use them again that they are calm, that they have practical solutions, that they are team players, that they don't fight with people just for the sake of fighting, that they are intent on making something happen, and that they have the respect of others in their firm and others in the business.

Obviously, you can't be a wimp and be a deal maker. If somebody smells that you can't manage the deal, it just won't work. You have to look like, act like, and be a manager of process, of information, of people. I think it comes pretty naturally with experience.

There are many variations of deal management. If the deal starts with one CEO talking to another CEO, and they really think this is a good combination, and they know the price range and other conditions, then one of them comes to me, and we'll talk: How much time do you think we have to get this done? What's reasonable? What are the next steps? Often the CEO says they'd like to get together a week from now and talk about the major issues. This process takes on a life of its own; it has its own schedule. I "staff" it. I get people in the firm who will be on the team, and we start looking at what we need to do in terms of diligence. We get the facts about whether we're buying or selling stock or assets and which subsidiaries hold these assets. We have a number of checklists for diligence, and we figure out the one that fits this situation and start there. You just start going, right away.

Deal Making After September 11

Before September 11, 2001, I would have said that consolidation is a process that is undeniable. You can't argue against it, except when it reduces competition to the point where the markets and regulators can't stand it. But consolidation and globalization go hand-in-hand, and the issue that is beginning to pop up is companies in other countries asking themselves how much of their investment they really want in the U.S. because we are going to be under siege for quite some time. That will change business.

Now, I still think we're on a path of simultaneous globalization and consolidation. I think Americans are becoming much more culturally sensitive in companies; they know they have to have locals running the businesses they own in other countries. They know they're not always going to have a common language. And they're adjusting to that.

The face of the world is going to be very, very diverse; the face of business is going to be very, very diverse – and increasingly so. So how does that affect deal making?

This increasing diversity makes deal making both far more complex and far more challenging because it's harder to identify the issues that really matter. There are issues that are hard because of language and cultural differences that don't really matter, and some that do, and it's hard to tell the difference, as we're just getting into this period. I think it's going to be extremely interesting and challenging to make the right decisions, to take the right risks, to trust the right people.

Mary Ann Jorgenson is the firmwide corporate practice coordinator and is a member of the firm's management committee. She focuses her practice on the representation of public and private companies in securities matters, mergers and acquisitions, tender offers, and contests for corporate control, venture capital, and other financing, executive compensation, and corporate governance issues. She has particular experience in corporate growth strategies, representing several local and national corporations in multimillion dollar transactions. Ms. Jorgenson's corporate experience is complemented by her active service as both counsel and advisor to the CEOs and boards of large and growing businesses; she currently serves as director of three public companies, as well as several private companies and charitable organizations. She is listed in The Best Lawyers In America.

Ms. Jorgenson also has significant international experience. She has served as counsel to the Czech Government on several privatization transactions, including selling large state-owned businesses to Western buyers, and has served as advisor to the Ministry of Privatization of the Czech Republic in the review of privatization proposals. Additionally, Ms. Jorgenson handles international transactions for domestic corporate clients.

Ms. Jorgenson chairs the Corporate Laws Committee of the American Bar Association and is the former chair of the Corporation Law Committee of the Ohio State Bar Association and the Securities Law Section and the Securities Law Institute of the Greater Cleveland Bar Association. She is a trustee of the Downtown Cleveland Partnership and chairs its Euclid Avenue Task Force, whose focus is the revitalization of Cleveland's main street. For 13 years she also served as a trustee (including chair for three years) of Great Lakes Theater Festival, a regional classic theater.

Ms. Jorgenson is admitted to practice in Ohio and New York.

WINNING THE PENNANT...IT ALL STARTS WITH THE RIGHT TEAM STRATEGY

SAM COLELLA

Versant Ventures

Managing Director

Agreeing to Play

I remember it vividly. We were making an acquisition of a company. We had all of the leverage, and the seller needed us desperately. My vice president of business development was a very tough negotiator and had extracted more than a pound of flesh out of the seller. As president of the company, I was presented with the final documents, and the CEO of the seller company asked to spend a few moments with me in private. He gave me the best piece of advice I've ever received. "You've won me, you own me, but you've taken away my heart," he said. Because he was a crucial part of the acquisition, and we wanted him and his team probably more than his assets, I felt we hadn't really won at all; we had actually lost. I went back to our vice president of business development and the lawyer who was working with us on the negotiations, and I asked them to figure a way of giving the seller a concession, so he and his team could leave feeling they had won also, or that they had been treated more fairly. We did come up with a compromise, and in the long run it paid off.

Mastering the art of deal making in today's marketplace isn't merely about selling an idea or persuading your competitor to see things from your perspective. It goes much deeper. Rather, it's about relationship management, a collaborative process of learning from others and negotiating a shared solution.

For me, as a venture capitalist, the most challenging part of doing a deal is recognizing the negotiation does not stop at the funding of the company. We must be careful to preserve relationships initiated during due diligence. The conclusion of the negotiation must be at a point where all parties feel they were treated fairly, that it was a win-win for all participants, and that they can move to the next phase of building the company with a positive relationship. Connecting emotionally and treating people with respect and honesty and in a straightforward manner can help establish your credibility, earning you the negotiating power you need to succeed in today's competitive environment.

In venture capital, the art of deal making is finding a match between the skills required in the new company and the strengths of the venture capital firm and the individual venture capitalist. If there is not a match, then there will never be a successful deal.

Having spent 20 years as an entrepreneur and operating executive and 17 years as a venture capitalist, I parlay my experience and knowledge into the role of company builder rather than investor. My philosophy is that if you build a great company, you will make a great rate of return. I have never considered myself a great stock picker, but I have good judgment in evaluating markets, technology, and people, and in assessing a business proposition.

You never have a perfect crystal ball, but I believe it is essential to be able to hypothesize the possible road map to success. None of the dozens of companies I have invested in had all of the resources, assets, talents, or capital required for success at the time of our initial investment. As early-stage venture capitalists, we believe it's our role to work in concert with the entrepreneurs and startup teams to obtain the necessary ingredients to build the company.

Spring Training

Prelude to the Deal: Due Diligence

"I wish I'd known early what I had to learn late." – Richie Ashburn

Before entering into negotiations on a deal, we engage in due diligence to attempt to obtain information about the critical variables for success. Obviously, the information acquired is imprecise and incomplete, which is one of the reasons venture capitalists assume a great deal of risk with potentially commensurate rates of return. Following is a checklist I have used over the years to help evaluate opportunities:

Market

Is there a need for the product or service? Is the market large, and will it grow at a substantial rate? Can the company establish a defensible market position? Can it achieve significant market share? Is there, or will there be, formidable competition? Is the sales cycle a serious hurdle?

Is this a market where a young startup company can succeed?

Organization

Are the founders knowledgeable about their market? Do they have experience in their market? Are they innovative, experienced and success-oriented? Do they have impressive track records? Do they have a capable CEO, or will we need to recruit one in the future? At what time will we need to bring in the CEO? Is the team capable of building a large company?

Products and Technology

Is the concept unique? Do they have a strong intellectual property position? Will the product satisfy the market's need? Is the R&D plan realistic and feasible? How risky is the plan? Is there proof of principle?

Business Model

Are the numbers realistic and achievable? Are the margins attractive? Are they believable? What are the capital requirements of the business? Have they assessed price elasticity, margin variability, and profit potential?

Operating Plan

Is the strategy well-conceived? Can they articulate the strategy? Do they understand the specific tactics and tasks to execute the plan? Are the projects, in terms of resources required, time allotment, and outcomes expected, realistic?

Financial Terms

What are the capital needs, paths to liquidity, and timing of liquidity? What is the capital structure? What are the valuation expectations? What are the comparables? Can the company be easily financed in the future?

Risks

Are there killer risks? What is the risk-reward ratio? Can they articulate the major risks?

We do our best to engage the team in a dialogue on all of these questions. We will also interview industry experts, potential advisors, and other experts. We do thorough reference checks on the team and try to find plenty of face time with the founders. In many cases, we will use knowledgeable members of the organizations we have already invested in. We expect management to make formal presentations and respond to our in-depth questions during due diligence. Sometimes we may use technical experts in fields where the technology is extremely complex.

Venture capitalists should prepare for negotiations and be thorough. The time of due diligence should not be rushed. Both parties must be comfortable with the facts, the situation, and how each perceives the opportunity.

Taking the Field

Structuring the Deal: Preparing Mentally

"Good hitters don't just go up and swing. They always have a plan. Call it an educated deduction. You visualize. You're like a good negotiator. You know what you have, you know what he has, then you try to work it out." – Dave Winfield

You must understand the position of the entrepreneurs (or the founders) and the most important issues from their side, their passions, their visions, and where they want to end up in the long term, as well as the short term. Then you will need to determine your position on each of those items and how it relates to the total potential success of the enterprise. Laying out those issues and determining where your starting and ending points are in a negotiation are essential.

You also need to assess the characteristics of the individuals you are negotiating with. Are these people who obviously like to negotiate, like to barter, like to have a give and take? Or, as in many cases I've seen, do they just want to hear your last and final offer? To determine the nature of the individuals, you must spend a lot of time with them before the negotiation. This is all part of evaluating whether these are people you want to work with and collaborate with in building a new company.

The people we deal with in venture capital are passionate, committed, ambitious, and driven. What they want to see is the same excitement and passion they feel for their proposition. For me, that's the starting point and the platform for being persuasive. We cannot be phony or superficial; it has to be real from the venture capitalist's standpoint. Entrepreneurs and founders can see right through a "salesy" approach that doesn't have a concrete basis. I discipline myself: If I cannot get excited and passionate about a prospect, then it is not the right company to invest in. That's the key to being persuasive.

In preparing for a negotiation, it is important that you set the stage by giving the other side plenty of evidence that you have done your homework, you understand the company's prospects, you understand the technology and the market, you have done your due diligence, and you have a clear-cut vision of where this company is going and how it can succeed. Don't make the mistake of jumping right in to valuation, terms and conditions, and the bottom line. Every negotiation must be staged, and the first stage is a recap of your conclusions regarding the business proposition. Many times I will draft a summary of our due diligence and perspective on the opportunity, showing them we have put the energy, time, and thought into their proposition and that we have given it serious consideration.

The Pitch

Putting the Deal Together: Deal Negotiations

"The first principle of contract negotiations is don't remind them of what you did in the past – tell them what you're going to do in the future." – Stan Musial

Assuming the due diligence is positive, we can begin negotiating with the founders to establish initial valuation, size of financing, magnitude of the employee stock option pool, and detailed terms and conditions. While there may be a willing buyer and seller, these negotiations can be extremely precarious. Since we will become active members of the board of directors and will be working with the entrepreneurs on a daily basis to build the company, we take special care not to damage our relationship during these deal negotiations. In all cases, there will be a bid and asking price, so negotiations will be spirited.

I can honestly say I do strive for a win-win situation in every deal. I want the team to be motivated and feel they were treated fairly. However, I have a fiduciary responsibility to our investors to make certain the terms and conditions reflect the status of the startup, its risks, and its upside potential, and that it is consistent with current market conditions. These are very high-risk endeavors, with a distinct possibility that they could end up being total failures.

Stealing Home

Handling Risk

"Any time you think you have the game conquered, the game will turn around and punch you right in the nose." – Mike Schmidt

Our business is fraught with risk. You can't take all of the risk out of the equation as an early-stage venture capitalist. Top-tier venture capitalists anticipate only 10 percent to 15 percent of their investments will be "home runs," and strike-outs could be as high as 20 percent to 25 percent. This fact requires venture capitalists to pay particular attention to valuation and ownership metrics and projections. We must also forecast future rounds of financing and project step-up valuations through the IPO and post-IPO. I have always felt great companies had to allow for each new investor to make a satisfactory rate of return, including those that bought on the IPO and after-market. This requires discipline in setting price-per-share targets and a constant "gut check" of the realistic assumptions for the future.

Some situations exist where you structure the deal on a staged financing, where a given amount of money is invested at the front end, and then upon meeting certain milestones, additional capital is put into the company. Many times these are done on a predetermined basis, where the milestones, the price-per-share, and the amount of capital to be invested are predetermined. In many cases, we will put only enough money in to reach the milestone and then negotiate the price and terms for the next phase. Quite often, it's a roll of the dice.

Regardless, you must have confidence in the individuals, believe in your due diligence, and be completely convinced in the capability to alter the course of action if necessary. It is rare when everything works according to the business plan, the executive summary, or the vision as originally stated by the entrepreneurs. This business is one of forever taking information, learning more, getting more information, and making adjustments throughout the life of the company.

Free Agents

Making the Sell: Choosing the Best

"I'm not concerned with your liking or disliking me ... All I ask is that you respect me as a human being." – Jackie Robinson

The venture capital business is competitive, and the best entrepreneurs will have multiple offers. Most often, entrepreneurs do not necessarily choose the highest offer. Today the best founders are experienced and skilled and do not look just for money, but for partners who can aid them in building their company. They look for venture capitalists who have strong track records, domain knowledge, and references who speak to their abilities and contributions. These founders want to find a lead investor who can put together a syndicate to finance the companies. Syndicates can be as small as two venture capital firms, but many times they are as large as four or five firms. In the very early stages, the venture capitalist may see the deal and do it alone to round out the team or the technology, or right the business plan. These are considered to be "seed" investments. I prefer to be the lead or co-lead of most of the companies I invest in because I prefer to be active in working with the companies, using my operating experience and background.

So, in approaching a negotiation, we must first sell the entrepreneur or founders that we can lead the deal and obtain the necessary financing for them through syndication or through our own funds. These discussions take place before getting into specific valuation terms and conditions. Entrepreneurs are looking for a number of characteristics in a lead venture capitalist, including investors who have "deep pockets" to invest in more than just the early rounds, but who can continue to participate in late-stage financings, up to the IPO. We leverage our position by working hard to convince the entrepreneurs and founders that we are value-added investors and that we bring more than money to the table, and then we offer our references, track record, and industry experience as evidence.

I think chemistry plays a big part in the final selection of the venture capitalist, as it does in the companies in which venture capitalists wish to invest. Founders must feel a kinship for their lead investors. At our firm, we provide entrepreneurs with our references, which is only fair since we ask them for theirs in the process period. We want them to call our portfolio companies and previous companies, as well as industry authorities, because it is quite different from investing in a public security, where the transaction has no human element. In startup venture capital, these are very personal situations requiring bonding because you are entering into a partnership that can last for many years. The human element plays a significant role in a successful negotiation. If the founders and venture capitalists are on the same wavelength, then it becomes an easier negotiation.

Three Strikes

Know When to Fold 'Em

"You can't win them all." – Connie Mack

On the other hand, negotiations can also go awry. So how do you know when to walk away from the deal? Parting is usually based on your inability to reach common ground on valuation, terms, or the vision for the business. I have also walked away from deals because during the negotiation process, I saw the true colors of the opposing party. Many times you see a different side to their character, which is best to recognize early and acknowledge before you're joined at the hips in this long and tedious process of building a company.

I refuse to become involved in situations where valuation or price is the only issue. While I recognize valuation is important because it reflects ownership, there is much more to building a successful company. In the end, if you build a successful company, having a few percent more or less ownership is inconsequential to your ultimate financial rewards. I attempt to make the negotiation simple and straightforward. I will not enter into an auction. While I recognize competition, I want to invest in companies looking for the best match in their venture capitalist, not just the best price.

Bottom of the Ninth, Bases Loaded

Go for Broke

When the final negotiations occur, they must be timely, precise, prompt, and not dragged out. I try to avoid the ping-pong type of negotiation where an offer is made, a counter offer comes back, and another offer is made, and so on.

Leaving the details to the lawyers, I like to establish the main issues to be resolved:

❏ Valuation (pre-money valuation)
❏ Size of the financing
❏ Post-money valuation
❏ Founder ownership position
❏ Size of the stock option pool
❏ Syndicate participation and their individual ownership requirements
❏ Liquidation provisions

Hitting a Home Run

Closing the Deal

"My job is to give my team a chance to win." – Nolan Ryan

I believe the win comes in a handshake when both parties are satisfied that they want to proceed to legal documents. In very few instances have I seen negotiations break down after a handshake. If you have done your preparation properly, if you have developed a rapport with the founders, the handshake is the bond.

If agreement can be reached, a venture capitalist typically produces a signed term sheet, incorporating the key elements, plus a few other details, and submits it to the company for approval and signature. The company and the investors both appoint counsel to hammer out the definitive documents over the next two to three weeks, which is followed by a closing, when the money is transferred to the portfolio company.

Then the fun begins! Everybody focuses on the task of building a great company. This is also the honeymoon period because everything seems to work. You have a vision. You have a plan. You have enthusiasm, and the company is well-financed.

Winning the Pennant

Keeping the Deal Together

"If things don't come easy, there is no premium on effort. There should be joy in the chase, zest in the pursuit." – Branch Rickey

The advice I find myself telling my team most often is to always remember the venture capital business is a service business. We are here to service the entrepreneurs, our portfolio companies, and our investors. As a service company, we pay attention to the needs of others. We must be open and forthright in how we bargain, consistent in what we say and write, and empathetic in how we treat each other. Each investment must be viewed as if it were your own company. It is a huge undertaking, an immense amount of work, an undertaking in which you will spend many hours and years, so you must be passionate about it.

You must believe in it. You must not have doubts. You really have to be convinced this is something you want to put your time into. Yes, you are investing money, but it is your crucial time that is the limiting item.

At the end of the day, deal making requires insight, preparation, compromise, and persistence. The successful deal maker adequately visualizes both sides' needs and requirements, listens with empathy to try to understand, asserts a position by demonstrating its benefits to everyone feeling its impact, and through this honest and direct approach, creates a "win-win" proposition for all parties involved.

Sam Colella is a managing director with Versant Ventures, a healthcare-focused venture capital firm investing in medical devices, biotechnology, and health technology companies. He is regularly quoted in stories about the biotech, genomic, bioinformatics, and other rising healthcare industries, and has appeared in articles in the Associated Press, Red Herring, Fast Company, San Francisco Chronicle, and San Jose Mercury News, among others.

A highly visible venture capitalist, respected particularly for his leadership in life sciences investing, Mr. Colella co-founded Versant Ventures following 20 years of successful operational roles in high technology industries and more than 17 years with Institutional Venture Partners (IVP). He joined IVP as a general partner in 1984 and launched the firm's Life Science Group in 1985, the first such focused group within a venture capital firm in the industry. With investments focused in medical devices, biotechnology, and e-health companies, Mr. Colella is credited with an extensive list of successful life science companies, including Onyx Pharmaceuticals (public), Vivus (public), Pharmacopoeia (public), CV Therapeutics (public), and Symyx Technologies (public).

Before IVP, Mr. Colella held a variety of operational positions at a broad array of diverse businesses, including president of Spectra-Physics, the world's leading laser supplier, and senior manager of the Technical Products Division of Corning Glass. His professional affiliations and honors include being elected director of the National Venture Capital Association, president of the Western Association of Venture Capitalists, and chairman of the American Entrepreneurs for Economic Growth. Mr.

Colella has a bachelor's degree in business and engineering from the University of Pittsburgh and an MBA from Stanford University.

THE POWER OF EXPERIENCE

JOSEPH A. HOFFMAN

Arter & Hadden

Partner and Chairman of the
Corporate/Securities Practice Group

Negotiating: More Than Making a Deal

One of my greatest strengths is the experience I have gained in more than 20 years of practice. As a corporate and securities lawyer during this entire period, I have represented large and small public and private companies, investment bankers, banks and financial institutions, venture capitalists and strategic buyers, and individuals in a wide range of transactions, including corporate finance and acquisition transactions, public and private mergers, spin-offs, stock and asset purchases, and all types of securities transactions, including public offerings by public companies to raise capital for acquisitions and initial public offerings (IPOs).

I enjoy the sense of accomplishment in successfully completing a transaction. A recent transaction involved a company that was buying another company in a $250-$300 million deal. The negotiations were progressing at a reasonable pace, but as the deadline approached, we literally were working around the clock to sign the deal within five days. It was not very pleasant at the time, but I felt a tremendous sense of accomplishment when my client was ecstatic that they achieved the deal they wanted in the time allotted.

In many transactions, the challenge of finding a middle ground on issues, being creative in solving problems, bridging different positions, listening to what people are saying, and trying to find solutions, while dealing with egos and emotions adds to the satisfaction of a job well done.

When representing sellers, there is often angst about third persons discovering that the subject company is for sale. The seller often prefers to keep the sale a secret until the last document is signed. CEOs can be egotistical and demanding. Negotiating means more that just making the deal; it also means dealing with all sides of the table, getting the representatives together, and making everyone happy and agreeable with the result. The goal is to reach a position that is realistic with terms and conditions with which both sides can live. In a previous transaction, a seller of a business would not negotiate certain terms of the deal until the documents were about to be finalized and signed because he hoped we would agree to his unfavorable conditions. When our client maintained its position, he finally relinquished and, because it would give our client the deal they wanted, we were instrumental in revising and documenting the amended deal. The seller was an extremely difficult person with whom to bargain, but to obtain the deal, we tolerated his difficult behavior, kept our eye on the goal, and completed the deal in our client's favor.

Shifting Perspectives

Perspectives are different, to some extent, among all the parties involved in a deal. As lawyers, we are focused on protecting the client, limiting their liability, negotiating for their protection, and requesting everything to which our client is entitled. Inexperienced lawyers may not know what issues to raise and points on which to insist when negotiating deals. As you gain experience, you learn to focus on legal and business issues that are key to the client. Attorneys should always strive to ensure all issues are adequately reviewed and covered.

Because venture capitalists and financial buyers invest their own money, they are cautious, focused on the business fundamentals, and centered on their returns. They want to be protected, have an exit strategy, and have a way to retrieve their money and maintain control. Some industry or strategic acquirers focus on getting the deal done. These companies also want legal protection, but they do not want to go overboard spending too much time on largely theoretical risks. Accordingly, a lawyer must be practical in the deal making process. From management's perspective, working on a deal takes time and focus away from running their business. Some companies have separate acquisition groups, but that is usually the exception, rather than the rule. Typically, it is the CEO or the CFO, or both, and other senior executives who are spending time away from the business, analyzing the target, reviewing documents and conducting negotiations.

From everyone's perspective, comprehensive negotiations and thorough due diligence at the beginning of a deal will avoid problems after the closing of a deal. Issues raised during the deal making process when everyone is working together, can be dealt with during the negotiations. If potential problems are overlooked and the deal is completed, issues may arise later, causing a contest between the parties. Clients do not like surprises or unforeseen problems. Accordingly, we seek to deal with problems and issues during the negotiations. Due diligence must be comprehensive. The due diligence process involves learning the client's business and encouraging issues to surface sooner rather than later.

Characteristics of a Great Deal Maker

A successful deal maker gets things done on time. Time kills deals. When situations linger, the parties involved may change their minds. A recent client we represented in an individual capacity was involved in a deal that was prolonged because the seller of the business wanted to postpone the deal for a few months to receive favorable tax treatments. Then the market crashed, and the deal never closed. The opportunity to sell at a good price was forfeited because of the one-month delay.

A successful deal maker gets things done, but sometimes the best deal is the one that does not get made. In the process of due diligence, sometimes unavoidable issues arise. In another earlier deal, the quality of the revenue of the acquisition target was not what we anticipated because of some questionable billing practices. We decided not to proceed with the transaction. Everyone was disappointed because no one likes a dead deal, but the CEO believed that the thorough due diligence and the decision not to proceed saved the company the $300 million purchase price.

A successful deal maker does not get lost in theoretical issues. The client needs protection, but the attorney must also be practical about possible consequences. A successful deal maker listens to his client and assumes his client's perspective.

Judging Success in a Deal

A deal is a success when it is completed on time, and the client is happy with the results. Success is negotiating a good deal for the client that meets the client's expectations. Success provides quality representation that covers all the relevant issues, protects the client, and provides agreement on the issues that are important to the client.

A couple of years ago, our client needed to raise some funds in the public markets for an acquisition of a company, but an underwriter withdrew because of its lack of confidence in the client's ability to raise the necessary funds. The time frame under which our client was working specified that if the acquisition was not completed at a given time, the client would have to pay an additional $500,000 in the purchase price for the company. The deadline was the end of September; a new underwriter was secured in July. The complicated underwritten public offering closed by mid-September, in a little over two months. Our client saved the $500,000, which, given the tight time schedule, the seller was expected to collect. That was a success!

Deal making is a little like a chess game, to some extent, especially when dealing with counsel that is also sophisticated and experienced in doing deals. Anticipation of all the issues that will arise and preparation to handle those issues mark the expertise of a true deal maker.

From a document standpoint, setting the framework by drafting the documents puts the client in a better position at the negotiating table. A common example, especially during purchase and sale transactions, is that the other side will try to reframe the contents in a way that is much more beneficial to their side's indemnification section of the transaction's documents. Cogent arguments and sound rationale make powerful arguments, and if credibility is developed in the process, people tend to listen.

Deal Making Challenges

From the lawyer's standpoint, one of the biggest challenges in making deals is supervising and coordinating all aspects of the deal. The corporate/securities attorney general directs, or "quarterbacks," all the parties – the firm's experts, the accounting firm, the client's company representatives, and the investment bankers. The challenge is keeping apprised of all aspects of the deal and making sure all comments are reviewed and appropriately reflected in the documents. Awareness of the various specialty areas – environmental, ERISA, labor law, tax law, and so on – is imperative. Coordination of the experts involved in the deal is essential.

The second challenge is performing quality work in a compressed time schedule. It is important to keep track of everything, to miss nothing, and to get everything done.

Sometimes multiple deals coincide. Each client likes to feel they are the only important client.

Another challenge includes parties with unreasonable expectations about price, timing, or realistic accomplishments. Most people tend to be reasonable, but once in a while, someone will have inflated ideas of what their company is worth, or they will take positions that are inflexible and unreasonable. When a party wants too much and cannot agree on a price, discipline is needed in the negotiation process to be able to say "no." Six months later, the party may return to renegotiate after they have investigated and discovered that no one was willing to pay them the amount our client was willing to pay them.

Financing challenges can kill deals. Here is a problem scenario: The performance of a company for sale starts trending downhill, and the potential buyer's financing source gets nervous. Maybe the buyer wants to negotiate, but the seller does not because he has an established price in his head. Even though the seller realizes the company is not performing as well as it was, he still thinks he should receive the same amount for it. The potential buyer's financing sources may become uncomfortable with a downward trend and withdraw.

The financing sources can also get uncomfortable with management. Honesty and integrity are expected and required. In an IPO deal a few years ago, the underwriters asked the CEO, our client, if there was anything in his past they should be aware of, and he said no. Then they conducted a background search and discovered he had pled guilty to some minor criminal offenses more than ten years ago and that he had declared personal bankruptcy. While none of this information was required to be disclosed in the prospectus under SEC rules, the underwriters felt there was a breach of trust. Even though the problems were more than ten years old, and the CEO had formed a new life and had been very successful in his new company, the underwriters withdrew. Had the CEO been totally candid with them, they probably would have completed the deal.

Gaining Leverage in a Deal

In large transactions, gaining the most up-front leverage when preparing the letter of intent is desirable. Many clients and business people tend to think the letter of intent is not very important because it is non-binding. Sometimes clients will not even have their lawyers look at the letter of intent. This is a crucial mistake. It is advantageous to have the attorneys review the letter of intent because they can suggest important issues to include in it.

If the client is selling his business, the letter of intent should include a limitation of the survival of the representations and warranties. For example, require that any action must be brought within 12 or 18 months after the deal, or it expires. A lawyer can often get some moral commitment in a non-binding letter of intent, so when preparing the definitive agreement, the parties are morally obligated to honor the letter of intent. It is difficult to "negotiate back," once a position has been discussed and tentatively agreed to. Leverage is weakened. Early involvement is necessary to obtain the greatest leverage. Always attempt to get clients, especially sellers, to negotiate a fairly detailed letter of intent that covers significant issues.

Also, look for provisions in documents that can result in gaining an upper hand later. Create a situation where the parties have to approach to have a discussion. I have seen attorneys notice a clear mistake in a document and not raise the issue until they need a concession later. They will return and say, "Well, we really need this, and by the way, here's a mistake that disadvantages you."

Leveraging a position with sound, creative arguments, gaining information regarding the other side, and predicting where they are planning to go with their negotiations strategy are advantageous. I remember reading years ago about a group who went to Japan to negotiate a deal. The first question they were asked by the other side was when their flight was leaving Japan to return home. The opposing side wanted to know what their time frame was. They refrained from the crucial negotiations until there was hardly any time remaining, so the people who were leaving felt constrained and at a disadvantage. Information is useful, especially when you have more information regarding the other side than they have regarding your side. Play cards close to the vest.

The correlation is leveraging a position by not being an open book and giving the other side too much information. In a transaction where we were selling a business for a client, the buyer stated, "It's our understanding that if you don't sell to us, you're going to liquidate." We would have been doing our client a disservice to acknowledge that fact, so we did not. Although the buyer may have suspected a liquidation alternative was true, they could not be certain.

Flinch or make a comment on a proposal from the other side, even if the client is totally accepting. Do not give the impression of being too eager. Always consult with the client before letting the other side know if the client agrees to the proposal.

Rules for Negotiating Deals

In negotiations, be honest, fair, and reasonable. Part of the negotiation process is building credibility. The real goal is to never take unfair advantage of anyone. It is a small world, and you can acquire a reputation for credibility in the community by being honest, up-front, fair, and reasonable. Do not insist on unreasonable points on either side of the table. Never try to "pull a fast one" by sneaking in changes. In one instance, a client insisted on an unimportant issue that would create work for the other side. This insistence harmed his credibility with the other side.

Avoid emotions. Anger and intimidation to make a point creates a disservice to all involved. The other party's willingness to cooperate and negotiate is often compromised.

Present the appearance of being in control and flexible on whether to do or not do the deal. To be most effective, be willing to walk away from the table. Be the custodian and drafter of documents to structure the contractual relationship to the best advantage of your client. If the other side is the drafter and specifies issues, arguments, and positions from scratch, they might raise issues about which they would be concerned. However, when they have to read a document or agreement prepared by us, they sometimes do not see what is "not" contained in the document or agreement.

Location of the negotiations can make a difference. Always negotiate on home turf to be comfortable and in control. In a recent deal, the seller wanted to negotiate in New York, but our client said no. Throughout the deal, we either met on the phone or in my office, so the seller was more inconvenienced. During the final crunch toward closing, they were not getting as much sleep as we were. Still, we worked around the clock to close within five days. It is always better to claim the "home court" advantage.

Technology is a great tool. Often, when working on a transaction with another law firm, we search a variety of databases for the last five deals the other firm has completed. We see the documents they have written and the points negotiated. There is so much information available now that taking a little time to look can formulate a good picture of the law firm's past negotiations. So when the firm says, "We never do that," we can counter with, "Well, what about the so-and-so deal, where you did...?" Doing homework and using information is advantageous. Knowledge is power.

Be an expert of the law. The client may discover too late, after his deal is done, that there were taxes or additional obligations due and payable by him, obligations that his lawyer did not mention.

In transactions, make sound, well grounded arguments. Know the points needed to win. Be confident, which comes with experience. Some attorneys may know the right answer, but if they are not confident and do not make the points as if they really believe them, the other side will not be convinced. Neither will their client. Adopt a reasonable approach, and avoid asking for points that are extraordinary or not customary. Negotiating for unreasonable points can cause a loss of credibility. Keep discussions on a friendly basis; do not allow discussions to get out of hand. Once a situation turns unfriendly or unprofessional, the situation tends to go downhill.

Assessing the Client's Risk – Risk Management

In helping clients assess risk, rely on experience with respect to problems that arose in the past, and be realistic about whether those problems will surface again. Often sharing risks with the other party aligns everyone's interests. If there is a shared risk, everyone will have the mindset to resolve the problem. If the risk is contained to one side, the other side may not cooperate or care to resolve the issue.

Several years ago, one of our clients sold a business, and there was a tax the buyers claimed my client owed on the sale. He disagreed, but to get the matter resolved, he said he would pay the tax and deal directly with the government. The government agreed with my client that he did not owe the tax. But he had a difficult time convincing the new owners to file an amended return because they had nothing to gain. My client finally had to "pound the table" and threaten a lawsuit. The result would have been much different, I suspect, if the parties had agreed to share the proceeds of the refund.

Another way to handle risk is through insurance. Our firm represents several insurance carriers that underwrite director and officer insurance, as well as representations and warranties insurance for merger, acquisition, and disposition transactions. Usually with an acquisition agreement, there are representations and warranties, and insurance can be purchased to cover certain breaches of the representations and warranties. If a seller wanted to be assured that they were selling their company, and that the purchaser could never come back to them for anything, the seller could spend the money at closing to buy a policy that would cover the risk. These insurance policies are underwritten, and depending on the size of the deal and the coverage, they can be expensive. But if certainty is a necessity in this situation, consider this kind of insurance.

Always try to shift the risk to the other side, whether they know it or not. This can be done creatively in the documents to gain leverage. To the extent that the other side has the risk when a problem arises, then they have to approach the negotiating table. Sometimes just refuse to accept certain risks. One approach we often use in acquisitions, especially when we are the buyer, is the "your-watch/my-watch" theory: If the problem happened while they owned the business, it was on their watch, so they should be responsible for it. This theory works in reverse when we own the business.

Best Advice

"Time kills deals." That phrase has a wide and frequent application. There is often only a small window of time to complete a transaction before market conditions change. Because it is hard to foresee the changes in market conditions, windows of opportunities open and close suddenly and without warning. A few years ago, we took public a golf equipment manufacturer. It was the largest IPO in the history of the country in the golf industry – a $110 million IPO. The company was performing well. Approximately a month after we completed the IPO, unforeseen by anyone working on the transaction, the golf equipment industry collapsed. Stock prices tanked, and everything went downhill from there. If the IPO had been delayed by only two months, the IPO might never have been completed.

Another client of ours was working for a seller of a business who wanted to delay the closing of a deal into the following year for tax reasons – they wanted to move the closing from the end of November to the beginning of January, just over a month. Unfortunately, the deal never closed. Instead of getting $6 or $7 million out of the deal, now they have a company that is basically on life support because market conditions changed, and the buyer became nervous, delayed the transaction further, and finally withdrew. The deal was killed the following April – all because the seller wanted to delay it for tax purposes.

The advice I give most frequently is: Do whatever it takes, within the bounds of ethics and the law, to meet the commitment. Our firm is committed to providing quality legal work, which can include working extended hours. Clients expect requests to be completed on a timely basis. We strive to meet or exceed the expectations of our clients.

My advice to anyone who wants to learn how to make deals is to find a mentor and learn to work on teams for his or her clients. Dive in and take ownership of projects. Read! An excellent book called *Anatomy of a Merger* by James C. Freund walks the reader through an acquisition agreement step-by-step. He was a senior partner at a well-known firm in New York. Many people have read his book and learned from his experiences.

Teamwork for Successful Deals

People who work on our teams have to take ownership and responsibility. In law firms, attorneys are the primary contact with their clients. Most of the clients I deal with are both friends and long-time business associates. When I ask another attorney to serve on a client team, I want him or her to take ownership of that client relationship and be as responsible for the same high-quality work for the client as they would for their own clients.

Having competent team members is critical. Clients pay a substantial amount of money for the legal services we provide. It has been our experience that when rendering services in a timely and competent manner, the client rarely questions the fees. But if your whole team has done a great job except for maybe one person, the client tends to focus on that one person. Their overall impression will be, "Yes, everything went great, except for this one person . . ." Everyone has to do their work and do whatever it takes to get the deal done. Our secretaries and administrative assistants are a very important part of our service. During a recent deal, two secretaries rotated while working 24 hours a day over a four-day period, and the clients really appreciated it. In a service business, this level of service showed an unwavering commitment to the client.

Golden Rules for Making Deals

❑ Be honest, fair, and reasonable, earning credibility in the process.

❑ Draft the documents.

❑ Control the situation.

❑ When hiring counsel to assist with deals, hire experienced people. If the deal is not within the expertise of the firm or attorneys, the client's interest is not served.

❑ Look for leverage points and opportunities for trade-offs.

❑ Have a negotiating game plan to get where the client needs to be.

❑ Think creatively in trying to solve problems. The object is not to beat up the opposition or make them look bad, but to achieve a win-win situation.

Making Deals in the Future

Deals are becoming more intricate and complex all the time. In a recent deal, the acquisition agreement was over 150 pages. True, it was a $250-300 million deal, but years ago, when I started my practice, a deal agreement would rarely be longer than 30 pages. Today, because there is easier access to information, especially online, and to all the bells and whistles used by attorneys, deals have become more complex. Consequently, deal agreements are more comprehensive. I believe this trend will continue.

Technology is becoming increasingly more important, because it shortens response times. We have a number of clients and lawyers who carry "Blackberries" with them when they travel, e-mailing each other instantly, even in meetings, being constantly in touch with everyone. Time frames for deals continue to be more compressed, largely because of this instant and constant contact.

Joseph A. Hoffman has been a corporate and securities attorney for more than 20 years and currently practices with the national law firm of Arter & Hadden LLP. His practice includes most areas of corporate and securities law, including mergers, acquisitions and dispositions, public and private offerings of securities, federal and state securities regulation, finance and venture capital financings, structured financings and securitizations, spin-

offs, and distribution and supply relationships. He graduated from The University of Texas at Austin, School of Law in 1981 (JD, with honors) and St. Vincent College, Latrobe, Pennsylvania, in 1978 (BA, summa cum laude).

Mr. Hoffman is a frequent speaker at seminars and has been a guest lecturer at the Edwin L. Cox School of Business, MBA Program. He co-authored (with Mark Solomon) the chapter "Securities Regulation" in the book Doing Business in Texas: A Guide for Foreign Investors Doing Business in the Lone Star State, published by the International Law Section, State Bar of Texas.

THE DEAL: MORE OFTEN THE BEGINNING THAN THE END

MARK J. MACENKA

Testa, Hurwitz & Thibeault

Partner and Chair of the Business Practice Group

Setting the Stage

I started out as a corporate associate at Testa, Hurwitz & Thibeault, LLP 18 years ago straight out of law school, and made partner in 1990. Our philosophy at our firm has always been to bring associates up through the ranks by providing them as broad a base as possible in terms of experience in representing businesses across a wide range of industries, including rapidly growing companies in emerging and high technology fields such as software, data networking and communication, the Internet, and life sciences. We see the life cycle of a business enterprise as a continuum and believe that a lawyer and deal maker should be experienced along the entire cycle. Clients expect us to understand the legal and business environments in which they operate, and they look to us as counselors, not simply as technicians.

My personal experience has followed that path. It's been helpful to make sure that over the years my experience includes representing companies at all stages of development and in all ranges of activities. I've represented two people in a garage with a business plan all the way up to large, multi-national, publicly traded corporations, and everything in between, including day-to-day business counseling, private and public financing, mergers and acquisitions, and complex commercial, licensing, and joint venture arrangements, both domestic and cross-border.

At the same time, we also gain experience representing those groups that bring capital to the table: the venture capitalists and private equity players. Like most of our Business Practice Group attorneys, I've represented venture capital funds, both as they make domestic and international portfolio investments in various high growth companies and in their own fund formation process. As a result of this breadth of experience, we are better able to understand what is going on in their thinking and their negotiations with their limited partners, who in turn are supplying the venture capital industry with the funds they use to invest in these companies. Whether we are representing the company or the investors in a deal, we can bring insight into what is motivating the other side and a thorough familiarity with deal terms and dynamics, and this experience enables us to resolve issues in an acceptable manner more quickly.

Along the way, we also represent the large investment banks in the capital-raising area, which includes initial public offerings and follow-on offerings, and in the merger and acquisition advisory area. Of course, our representation of companies keeps pace with their growth and also includes public offering and M&A work, both domestic and cross-border. On the company and investment banking sides of the equation, we've focused on bringing hundreds of companies public over the years. In the M&A area our practice encompasses transactions on both the buy side and the sell side.

This background enables us, having represented and worked with all the different types of players at different times in the past, to bring a lot more perspective to every transaction. By understanding what is motivating our client and the person on the other side of the table, by being thoroughly familiar with the range of business and legal deal terms and possibilities, and by having a wealth of experience in deal dynamics through having worked with players in different roles in various types of deals, I believe we have a better chance of achieving the goal of getting a deal done successfully. By combining a deep understanding of a client's business environment with exceptional legal advice, an attorney can provide value-added counsel and advocacy that extend beyond just giving the "right" technical advice.

Scoping Out the Deal

The first thing a deal maker needs to do is understand what your or your client's goals are and what the participants want to get out of the particular deal at hand. Part of that is identifying, among the owners and managers, who the decision-makers are and who will call the shots and decide what the appetite is for compromise. It's also important to get a full sense of the leverage you bring to the table. You must go through the same exercise with the opposite side, figuring out their goals and their reasons for being at the table. Make sure you can identify who their decision-makers are, whether it's the people at the table, people back at the office who can second-guess decisions that are made during the negotiations, or, the worst of all, a committee, which can add a lot of time to the process. Understand as much as you can about their appetite for compromise and what kind of leverage they bring to the table. It's important to understand who may hold more cards and who ultimately can exercise more leverage in the negotiations.

The way to prepare for a deal varies depending on the subject matter, but in general, I read as much as possible about the other side and try to understand their level of development, whether they're a startup or a venture-backed operation or a large, publicly traded company. To some extent, you can find a lot of the information on the Web: cash position, who their investors are, who is on their board of directors, what deals they have done before. It is important to understand, for example, if it is a product deal, where they need some of your client's technology, how important that product or technology is to their development efforts and their build-or-buy decision, and whether there is a second source out there on the market. If it's in the merger and acquisition context, find out which party needs the deal more, what their needs are, and whether they are cash-constrained or cash-rich. At this point, the deal is about strategic issues, non-legal issues, finding out who your opponent is and what motivations could be driving them.

The Art of Compromise

Many qualities and skills make a good deal maker. A basic quality that often goes unnoticed is common sense. It's critical. A basic skill is the ability to listen and to be self-aware of the position you are taking and the impression you are giving. Those are talents a person brings to the table that are built over years of experience. Another requisite for doing a deal well is being very experienced in the subject matter at hand, whether it's mergers and acquisitions, or public offerings, or venture capital financing, or complex commercial, licensing, or joint development arrangements. You need to have command of the issues and the possibilities and be willing to give concrete advice and direction. You need to have been there before, so you can understand what is "within the realm of standard" versus what may be out in left field. Also, so much of deal making is the art of compromise, and to be skilled at that, you have to have a thorough command of the issues and a big reserve of experience.

As I said before, it is important to understand what is motivating each side to do the deal. In identifying the goals of your client or your team and the goals of the other side, a successful deal maker must first develop an understanding of whether getting this particular deal done is the end in itself. Once you put the deal to bed, each side can go off and do something else, or, alternatively, it can be the beginning of a long-term relationship. More often than not, it's the latter.

Getting the deal done is not the end of the process, but the beginning of the process. So if it's the beginning, one of goals of getting the deal done is not only to get an optimal solution for your own client, but to understand that part of that optimal solution is making the other side successful, as well. The art of compromise is understanding that many opportunities are win-win, and that doing deals is a far cry from a zero-sum game. Part of the challenge is trying to figure out areas of commonality. The art of compromise is realizing that it is not always necessary to give in or cave in or horse trade, which I don't necessarily think is a good way to get to the end. But an essential skill is being able to take a step back and understand what both sides are trying to get at. If you stay too much in the weeds or focus too much on the particular provision being negotiated, you may miss an opportunity to move the ball forward and make great gains. Taking the time to step back and approach the problem from a different angle can lead you to suggest a solution that wasn't apparent because the hours of discussions that led to this point were approaching it from another angle. Just stopping, taking a breath, stepping back, and suggesting alternatives can be very helpful.

In my mind, the most persuasive negotiators can clearly articulate the reasoning behind the point they are making, as well as acknowledge the concerns the other side has. They are willing to make a decision and concede points, but only after determining why it's not a big issue in the first place. The most persuasive negotiators hit all the issues – not only their own, but the other side's, as well – and explain why those concerns pale in comparison or, while acknowledging their importance, demonstrate why those concerns are satisfied through other provisions or protections. By providing a reasoned explanation or rationale for their position, then even if they then discount the concerns of the other side and point out why such concerns aren't sufficiently compelling, or why those concerns are satisfied through other protections, it tends to be easier to resolve than if they just flatly said no.

When a rationale is clearly articulated and is not dismissive of the other side's concerns, it becomes easier to arrive at a compromise that can satisfy the concerns of both sides. If you are able to identify the other side's real concern, then it becomes easier to offer another alternative for protection that is tailored to that concern, while still being able to give your client what they need. This skill goes back to having deep and broad experience in the subject matter of the deal and being in command of the various terms and alternatives that can be suggested as compromises, as well as the ability to be able to take a step back to understand what the other side needs.

Success = Building Partnerships

Assuming both parties view this deal as the beginning of a relationship, it is important that both sides feel they were successful in building a relationship that can carry them forward in a mutually satisfactory and profitable way. You can't get overly ambitious and negotiate such a deal for your client that the other side wakes up a month or six months later and realizes they really got the short end of the stick. Part of successful deal making is helping your client see six, 12, or 24 months down the road, so they can understand where they may be and what situations they may be facing. It's giving the kind of advice that enables your client to see around the corner. By allowing them to see farther down the road, you can often help them come up with a position that is more acceptable to both sides.

The art of deal making is a combination of preparation, understanding the facts and the issues, employing leverage and experience judiciously, and tempering advice with practical suggestions and business savvy to make sure you don't let legal points drive the deal. You have to make sure that ultimately the deal is workable and is going to give the client and the business partner the outcome that they want. It's always focusing on the ultimate goal of the client and what they're trying to get out of it, and always trying to move the ball to that goal. That doesn't necessarily mean identifying the 36 key issues or the 12 key issues and knocking each of them off one by one. It's understanding that you're building a successful partnership, and you'll have to give in on some of these things. That's a skill. It's an art. You can't find what points you give in on and which facts you hold on to in a treatise or on a bookshelf; it's very fact- and circumstance-specific, and the issues and solutions change from deal to deal.

At all points, you want to preserve a way out. In doing so, you want to avoid things like "nevers," "non-negotiables," and "must haves." And you want to always be able to give a hook for the other side to hang their hat on, a way of saving face. After you fully understand and persuasively communicate the business issues that are driving the other side and those that are driving your side and then propose a solution, you want to make sure you provide a graceful exit to allow the other side to save face and get on to the next point. This is particularly useful if the business person on the other side finds your rationale or justification compelling, and you now need to bring their lawyer around.

One situation I try to avoid is where one businessperson talks to a lawyer, and the other businessperson talks to a lawyer, and the two lawyers speak. Unless it's a very good deal maker lawyer who understands the issues, the last thing you want to do is engage in a discussion when people don't have the authority to concede or compromise on a point. All that does is add a three-hour conversation so they can transcribe comments and give them to their client. The more that is at stake, the bigger the deal, the more critical it is that everyone gets together in the same room, or at least in the same phone conversation. You want to make sure the business people can hear the rationale behind every point. Most of the points you end up sticking on are very important to both companies, and they need to understand the motivations driving these decisions. Very often in direct interaction, after you have framed the issues, the business people are able to arrive at a compromise much more quickly than if the bid-and-ask is translated back and forth between two lawyers.

In my view, the difference between good deal makers and great deal makers is that great deal makers, while they get the optimal deal for their client, also figure out how to make both sides walk away from the table thinking they got their cake and ate it too. There are some very good deal makers who are more slash-and-burn types. They come in and really beat you up, and they can get a good result for their client. It's not the wrong way to approach things, but an even better result is getting a good deal for yourself, as well as the other side, which can often yield tangible and intangible dividends well into the future. Ultimately, whether or not it is a good deal, there is so much goodwill generated from the deal making and relationship-building process, that it sends the business people off on a very good note. The deals from which I exit shaking my head in appreciation are the ones where the other side has left happy, too. There are some large deal-doing companies who have this nailed, who have good business development teams and lawyers who work with them who understand how to go in and motivate the seller of a business and make the management team feel wonderful about it. They also understand how to negotiate the deal well. Being good at it is making sure you get what your client needs, but also understanding what the other side needs to make things go smoothly.

Caution: Dozens of Moving Parts

It's important to identify the various constituencies within a client's organization and make sure they are properly prepared for what to expect. Management may actually be multiple constituencies. For example, the CEO, the CFO, sales, and engineering may all have separate stakes and points of view. Another group to consider is the board of directors, and there can be multiple constituencies there, as well. Venture-backed clients or venture-capital investors have one way of looking at things, and a corporate investor on the board, for example, may have a different set of motivations they bring to the table. You must also consider the client's other professional advisors, such as investment bankers and accountants who may play significant roles in the transaction.

We spend time getting our clients to tell us what is driving them in the particular transaction to better understand how active various constituencies may be in the deal. For example, if it's a merger, the board is certainly going to be active, and there may be an independent committee set up. We will need to sit down with them and find out their perspective and what is driving the basis for the deal in their minds. The dynamic of who is truly sitting at the table can vary greatly depending on, for example, whether it's a technology licensing deal or a large acquisition or sale of the company. Each of these constituencies also needs to understand the process and what to expect. Having a basic understanding and comfort level with the process helps them to buy in to the result.

You also can't neglect basic preparation. There's always a document at hand – a term sheet you're negotiating or a merger agreement or a financing document – that you must be fully familiar with, as well as with the prior deals that either party has done, particularly if they are public. You don't want to make a statement, and then have the other side pull up a deal your client has already done that contradicts your position. Although there are certain ways to try to deal with the other side calling you on something, such as saying that the client's corporate policy has changed since the time of the cited prior deal, it's better to avoid the situation altogether.

An important strategy while negotiations are ongoing is to have key team players remain focused on identifying and developing alternatives to the deal at hand. Creating viable alternatives, which may simply be a clear willingness to go it alone, not only adds to your leverage in negotiations, but the possibility of following another path can also serve as a catalyst for generating a sense of urgency in the other side and moving the current deal forward more rapidly. Even if, in reality, viable alternatives are long shots or at very early stages, it is helpful to create the impression that the deal being negotiated is not your only alternative. Keep in mind that the lawyers, the investment bankers, or the judicious use of a board member, can be helpful in this process.

When negotiating, it is important to listen to what the other side has to say. In my view, it's important that everybody understands the business or legal needs behind each comment. Try not to use non-negotiables, because deals develop and evolve, and the decision-makers you represent, whether or not they're at the table, can often come back and compromise on a point you may have pitched as being non-negotiable. If they want to negotiate, it undermines your credibility.

It is important to know when it's time to settle or give in on your position. Part of this is to realize the importance of listening and being aware of what is happening at the table. You learn a great deal from the negotiating tactics of the other side. Some negotiators are very straightforward and constantly look for compromises to help get a deal done. If they search out compromises nine out of nine times, and on the tenth time, they say that this point is established corporate policy, and they can't negotiate it, you could look through prior examples of deals they have done and realize they have never given in on this point. If I've done my homework and pulled down the prior deals to the extent that they are publicly available, I can have an associate quickly look through and vouch that that is indeed the case.

Situations can escalate at times, and if, for example, the CEO at the other side of the table seems fairly set in his or her ways, you can take a break and discuss that dynamic with your client. You have to take the temperature of the other side at different times throughout the process and constantly suggest alternatives or compromises. That is when it's important to have command of the issues and a broad base of experience behind you, so you can constantly approach issues from different angles and suggest compromises or alternatives. If you continue to run up against the same point, and the other side is able to articulate a valid business or legal reason they need to stick on that point, then perhaps it is time to leave that behind and go forward. Again, you have to talk to your own client and understand whether it is something they can ultimately live with.

There are different methodologies for managing a deal, depending on whether it's a merger, a venture-capital financing or a technology licensing agreement. It is important to make sure your support team is in place, not only across levels of seniority, but also across disciplines. You cannot underestimate the importance of specialists who know how their particular expertise fits into the overall deal, and who also understand their advice needs to be tempered by practical suggestions and business savvy tailored to the specific circumstances at hand. This approach enables the team to better provide comprehensive, integrated legal and business solutions.

Doing a deal involves not just the negotiations, but a lot of planning and execution with a myriad of details, as well. For example, in almost every deal heavy due diligence is needed to investigate whether, among other things, there are other material agreements that affect the transaction in important ways. It's critical to make sure you line up the team and that you have both business people and legal people who can do the due diligence and review the appropriate agreements. There are many, many moving pieces at this level, as well, that involve not just the negotiations, but also bringing in tax or intellectual property or litigation people or other experts who act as consultants and strategic advisors, and it is important to make sure everyone is on the same page. When you have three dozen moving parts, you have to make sure all those parts are being moved down the field at the same rate, so you don't wake up, having finally struck a deal, and realize all these other pieces need to be put in place before it can get done.

Taking Command of a Deal

It's important to identify the main points of contact on the two sides. Ideally, it's the lawyers and single business contacts, and then the goal is to constantly keep in touch with your own business contact to make sure you are on the same page as to what is being communicated and to touch base frequently as to tactics and strategy. To the extent there are other areas of contact, such as investment bankers, you have to continue to coordinate updates. For example, separate tax negotiations can be conducted concurrently with the business negotiations, while the diligence process continues on a somewhat independent basis. As deal manager, you need to constantly keep in touch to make sure everything is moving forward on a coordinated and consistent basis, and the work is being done well and on time. A lot of people are at your command, and you have to make sure everyone is getting the job done and funneling communications through the main contact people.

The team is everything. There are so many aspects to larger deals that you need many people behind you to make sure everything gets done well and on time. Matching the level of experience appropriately to the corresponding level of need is important to make sure the deal is done correctly and at a reasonable cost. You don't want to plan for people at a high billing rate to be doing diligence, and if you plan properly, you will be able to get the right level of expertise applied at the right level. Having a team of smart people who are well trained and have a good attitude means you can respond quickly and turn on a dime. You can negotiate multi-billion dollar deals in days, if need be, and make sure every issue is put to bed in the proper order.

This process doesn't just happen when you get the initial phone call regarding a deal from the client; this process is an inextricable part of the whole fabric of our business of providing legal services. It starts from day one and requires constant training and education, constantly giving attorneys direct experience in a multitude of deal situations beginning at a very early stage in their development. Having represented a wide range of business enterprises in your early years of development is important. You have to build that experience slowly. The base for doing an exceptional job on a deal is set months and years ahead of time.

The management of risk comes in at a variety of levels. The most urgent risk is that of getting the deal done or losing it. That overarching risk is always there. It's important to understand at a very early stage the needs of the client and the alternatives available to the client if the deal does not get done. Whether the client has viable alternatives goes a long way in determining whether the team has leverage or not. Whether you should compromise or concede has a lot to do with how important the deal is for your client and how many alternatives you may have. On that level, it's important to constantly keep in touch with the constituencies you've identified and for your client to understand what their appetite is to continue to negotiate or whether there are other alternatives available.

While doing any deal, the prime risk is the passage of time. You never know what's going to happen tomorrow, whether it's something with your client, the business of the other side, a competitor, or the economy as a whole.

There's a constant risk of an unforeseen event happening that could derail negotiations. In any transaction we face, there is always a press to do it as fast as possible to minimize the risk of the unexpected. For example, any of our clients could in theory be subject to a lawsuit or a claim that their intellectual property infringes that of another company. One of those letters can come out of the blue any day of the year. You can never know what tomorrow might bring, so there is always pressure to get the deal done as fast as possible.

So much of preparation relates to rapidly identifying and bringing to bear the appropriate resources so you can provide the highest quality of legal services on a timely basis. It's important to be able to turn on a dime, to provide expertise across a range of competencies and disciplines, such as business advice, tax advice, intellectual property analysis and litigation risk analysis, and to be able to bring that expertise to the table right away, deal with the issues, and keep the process moving.

Advice From the Trenches

You could have the best written contract or merger agreement or legal document, but if you don't have an effective remedy, the agreement may not be worth much. One of the things I constantly think about – and tell my associates to think about is – What is the remedy? And is it an effective remedy? Every legal document is a binding agreement. The whole reason you're doing a deal is to get the other side to agree to do something – to affect a merger or a distribution arrangement or to hand over a lot of money. Every deal has immediate and ongoing obligations for both parties. The question is, What is the remedy if the other person intentionally breaches or simply is unable to perform for reasons entirely outside their control? And by remedies, I don't mean only lawsuit claims. Very often litigation is not an effective remedy for the issue at hand because of the timing or the cost, or because the client actually wants to affect conduct, not necessarily receive damages. Effective remedies may include simply getting a seat at the negotiating table or making the situation unfavorable for a third-party interloper.

Another piece of advice is to continually take a step back and listen to what your client or the other side is trying to get at. Think outside the box. Think of different approaches, and suggest alternative ways of looking at or tackling a problem. Often you can find common ground by approaching a problem in a slightly different way.

As I said before, a key piece of deal advice is to fully understand what your client wants out of the deal. Don't get caught up in a lot of provisions or the wrong deal point. Make sure you explain to the client, if necessary, how the specific provisions of the agreement affect the overall objectives. For example, in a venture capital investment, many of the entrepreneurs and management people are very concerned about ownership percentage, without realizing they may be ceding control of the enterprise through other contractual techniques, such as restrictive covenants or voting agreements that make their ownership percentage irrelevant in an analysis of control. You must remind the client that without capital, their idea will never become a reality, or worse, someone else may beat them to the punch. It's much more important to get the capital and get the deal done in some realm of acceptability, and not hang on to issues that are of less importance. Understand you will have to give in on points, but at the end of the day, what is most important is to get the deal done. If you're successful in this, then your client is empowered to do what they set out to do: manufacture a product, employ people, build a business, and carry on their dream. To do so, there are certain things on which you and they will have to compromise.

Nothing beats experience, so you always have to keep yourself on the frontline. You can't be an armchair quarterback. If you turn yourself into an advisor or consultant, so you are available only to answer questions, that's fine, but you keep your edge by actually being in the deal. I continue to do deals because I enjoy being an active player in the trenches. Another thing you have to keep up on is general developments in the industry, not just legal changes, but business changes, too. Keeping track of other deals and legal developments is continuing education and is an essential part of the job. Finally, you look for ways to share the experience with other top practitioners. That can be outside of the firm through bar association meetings, but we also do a lot of work internally to make sure we leverage experience across the firm. We have frequent internal seminars and discussion groups with senior associates and partners on sharing deal experience, for example, focusing on mergers and acquisitions, financings, or complex licensing deals. We have brown-bag lunches to share war stories or talk about issues and current developments. It's a combination of actively doing deals, continuing legal education, and making sure you leverage the experience from across a broad practice of not only business lawyers, but lawyers in other practice groups, as well.

In my view, the golden rules of deal making include:

❏ Never lose focus on your client's goals.
❏ A better outcome for your client is not only getting an optimal deal for the client, but also getting a deal the other side is happy with.
❏ Avoid absolutes, and always leave a way out both for yourself and the other side.
❏ Never lose your temper unless you've planned to lose your temper.
❏ Keep the lines of communication open with your client and their other advisors.
❏ Always keep your team informed and motivated.

Faster Pace, More Expertise

Deal making will continue to change. You can see deal timelines have accelerated in the past, and now with e-mail communication, the timing of deals becomes even more accelerated. The faster pace forces everyone to make sure all the bases are being touched, and every issue is dealt with in real time. As timelines gets compressed, the amount of work that needs to be done doesn't change. There will be increasing pressure to make sure you have the right amount of expertise you can bring to bear at a moment's notice to knock all the issues off on a timely basis.

A recent trend we have seen is rooted in the proliferation of businesses in the late 1990s that brought management teams who didn't have much deal-doing experience. Deals tended to be more difficult because you had a lot of people who hadn't done them before. We are already seeing a re-focusing on seasoned and experienced executives and management teams. So while pressures to compress deal timelines will continue, as more seasoned and experienced managers are brought on board, you're more likely to get to a mutually acceptable ending sooner than you might have in the recent past.

Mark J. Macenka is a partner and chair of the Business Practice Group of Testa, Hurwitz & Thibeault, LLP in Boston, Massachusetts. Testa, Hurwitz & Thibeault, LLP is one of the fastest growing and most dynamic law firms in the United States. Founded in 1973, the firm has more than 400 lawyers in Boston. The firm's practice encompasses all principal areas of law affecting businesses and receives particular national recognition for leadership in the emerging technology and private equity and venture capital communities.

Mr. Macenka practices in the areas of business and securities law, representing public and private growth-oriented companies in emerging and high technology industries. His experience includes business counseling, mergers and acquisitions, public and private financing, software, telecommunications, Internet and technology licensing and distribution arrangements, strategic partnerships and joint ventures, and intellectual property. Mr. Macenka represents underwriters in public software, telecommunications, hardware, Internet, and information technology offerings. He also represents venture capital and other private equity funds in financing of portfolio companies.

Mr. Macenka received his BA, magna cum laude, from Georgetown University in 1980 and his JD from Harvard University Law School in 1983. Mr. Macenka is admitted to the Massachusetts bar (1983).

SUCCESSFUL DEAL DOING

PATRICK ENNIS

ARCH Venture Partners

Partner

Early Stages: Lots of Face Time Needed

Deal making is an art, not just a set of guidelines to follow. It is certainly not solely about getting the best financial terms. It is about understanding all the elements involved: personalities of the team, changing markets, recruiting environment, technology landscape, legal structures, and so on. You have to keep everything in mind at all times and, more importantly, stay in tune with any changing circumstances of the negotiations.

When we enter a deal, we are typically present at the earliest stages of innovation, often when the company doesn't even exist yet. A university professor or a national laboratory scientist has a great technical idea and wants to put a company together. Most of the time upfront is spent understanding the possibilities of the research and potential business applications. So at that stage, very little time is spent worrying about financial terms or the legal structure of the eventual transaction.

Forming a great startup involves many important steps that must be satisfied before an actual venture capital financing deal is consummated. These steps include finding and recognizing world-class science, ensuring the science has useful technological applications, convincing yourself the technology can be incorporated into practical products, and, of course, thinking all the time about potential markets for such products. Only when the founders and I have gone through these steps do we begin to focus our discussion on financial terms and stock terms. The early stages of these technology VC deals are often characterized by discussions among a very small group of people who know one another well and respect one other. And the negotiations are almost anticlimactic when compared with all the hard work that was accomplished leading up to the final negotiations regarding financial terms and legal structure. So in a sense, these "deals" have very little in common with classic Wall Street financial deals we see in movies or on television.

After the deal is finalized, the hard work really begins as the company starts on its journey. Typically, it can be anywhere from three to seven years for an IPO or M&A exit; remember we are dealing with raw, seed-stage technology startups. So the financing deal is not a climax; rather, it is an entry ticket to the arena in which the startup has to execute its business plan. Most startups, rather than pausing and reflecting and celebrating the closing of a deal, are more likely to be found working immediately on recruiting new team members and building the business. Such is the nature of great entrepreneurs.

One of the biggest challenges in deal making is making sure everyone feels they have been treated fairly while closing the deal on favorable terms for all parties. I have a fiduciary responsibility to my limited partners to get fair terms when I negotiate a deal. But at the same time, I can't have the other party walk away thinking they got the short end of the stick.

How do you depersonalize these negotiations when they are inherently personal? Because of the long time frame from seed-stage company formation to liquidity event, a venture capitalist will spend a lot of time with the founders as the months and years go by and doesn't want to poison the relationship (or sow the seeds for a future poisoning) by having a spat early on. Of course, one way to try to avoid that is to let the lawyers handle contentious issues, although that is often no solution, as the fine points of the negotiation need to be understood and agreed upon by the actual principals in the deal: the entrepreneur and the venture capitalist. Having an intermediary such as an attorney can be a copout and often creates more difficulties and can waste an enormous amount of time. So the best way to depersonalize conflict is to ensure the negotiating process is agreed upon *a priori*. Having a framework to come to an equitable conclusion can really help facilitate a deal. A key is to always keep momentum and progress during the negotiations. Sometimes it occurs in fits and starts. It is safe to have a period of time pass with nothing accomplished, as long as, on average, both sides feel a happy conclusion is imminent.

As I will mention often, it is very important to begin to build a good relationship with the entrepreneur from the beginning. After the deal is signed, there will certainly be plenty of time to become close, as I typically talk with the entrepreneur almost every day, for months and then years. However, it is important to spend a lot of professional and personal time with the entrepreneur before the deal closes. This will help speed things along during the deal negotiations and more importantly, will provide both sides with plenty of unvarnished data on the personal and professional likes, dislikes, strengths, weaknesses, and quirks. If there are irreconcilable differences, it is far better to discover them before the deal closes. If the match isn't close to perfect, it is often better to walk away and find another opportunity.

Other deal making challenges can arise depending on the current business climate. During the unprecedented technology startup boom that occurred in the late 1990s, one of the more challenging aspects was getting the deal done before someone else swooped down and put in a counteroffer. There existed a time pressure that normally did not exist in the entrepreneurial and venture capital world. Things are back to normal now, although many people don't realize it is "normal" because their only reference point was the late 1990s – a period of the sort we may not see for another generation, if ever.

During this go-go period, venture deals started to resemble Wall Street transactions. It was an interesting time in the VC industry. There are great anecdotes about VCs and entrepreneurs about to sign the documents at a closing dinner, when a competing venture capitalist, disguised as a waiter, would bring a new term sheet to the dinner table and try to win the deal at the last minute. Sometimes these folks were not entirely forthcoming, but it can take a while to figure out what is real and what is a mirage. The confusion and uncertainty often would freeze the current deal long enough to have changing circumstances torpedo the whole deal.

Since the venture capital markets began to rationalize in the 2000-2001 time period, deals have been conducted under much healthier circumstances – that is, a more stable and logical environment that allows for meaningful long-term growth and value creation. Most great companies and great fortunes are built slowly with a lot of hard work. Historically, there are very few overnight successes, but in the late 1990s, there were many temporary overnight successes. If you look back now, you will realize most of those "successes" are no longer around.

From a technology perspective, one thing about doing deals today that is very different from doing deals 20 years ago is the current ubiquity of personal computers. Back then, every time we changed a scenario in the business case, we had to take a break while people worked the new numbers out. Now we sit in negotiations with our computers in front of us, working with a spreadsheet in real time. God bless Microsoft Excel. Now we don't have to argue during a deal negotiation; we can just try the scenario.

Perhaps in the future the process of doing deals will become less personal because of reluctant travelers and a reliance on videoconferencing. I do not see that as a factor in early-stage venture capital, however, as the personal aspects are as important as ever. In addition, a successful venture capitalist should do about two new deals a year, limited by time and a practical number of boards a venture capitalist can serve on.

Successful VCs are not transaction-focused; rather, they are company builders who need to spend a lot of time with new companies, especially during the first two years. This amount of time can range from five hours a week to 40 hours a week per company, depending on the situation. Such intense value cannot be provided continuously via videoconferencing. A venture capitalist must invest the time and travel to be face-to-face with the entrepreneurs.

Preparing for a Deal

Ideally, the best preparation for a deal is to go into it with an existing personal or professional relationship with the other parties involved in the deal. Please note I resist using the popular phrase "other side of the table" to refer to the other parties in the deal. As I repeatedly emphasize, successful early-stage venture-capital negotiations are all about building and preserving long-term positive relationships. The phrase "other side of the table" implies winners and losers and focuses the attention on the deal mechanics. For early-stage venture capital, the focus always needs to be on long-term value creation, which occurs only as a by-product of building great, unique, and innovative companies.

At our firm, we often have existing relationships with the other parties involved in the deal. For instance, all of us are formerly either entrepreneurs, business people, or scientists or various combinations thereof. Most of my career, before I joined the venture capital profession, was spent in the worlds of science, engineering, product development, and marketing. I wasn't focused solely on financial transactions or subtleties of the law; I was more focused on products and innovation. So now when I negotiate a deal in a venture capital transaction, I have credibility and a lot in common with the entrepreneur and the other folks involved. To me that is a great strength, one that is much more important than being able to negotiate the last dollar in a deal.

I do early-stage venture capital, where nobody knows the exact value of the transaction. These are not later-stage companies where you can measure the cash flows down to the nearest cent. So it is really not so important that you strike the best financial terms; more important is that you strike the best terms that will allow the company to grow, and then when the company is a billion-dollar company in several years, everyone will be happy. Even if you have a perfect transaction – when you have negotiated that final cent, which is often what they teach you on Wall Street and in business school – you may have blown the relationship, which may poison the working relationship going forward.

Doing a venture deal is like getting married. It is a three- to seven-year time horizon before the financial exit. So you need to ensure mutual trust and respect. The entrepreneurs we work with enjoy working with us because we had a great deal of real-world experience in science, technology, and business before we entered the venture capital profession. Frankly, many technology entrepreneurs have a healthy disdain for cookie-cutter VCs who have never worked in a lab, developed a real product, or managed a real business. Entrepreneurs usually don't respect investment banking or consulting experience. The entrepreneurs may be polite and not let you know that; but trust me, savvy entrepreneurs can size up VCs very quickly.

When you are an early-stage venture capitalist, your personal and professional lives are heavily mixed together. Many of my close personal friends are people I work with and vice versa. There are many reasons for this. Some of it is self-selection, *e.g.,* the folks who go to Wharton for an MBA or Yale for a Ph.D. in physics tend to get involved in interesting endeavors as the years go by. Since I spent time at both those institutions, my personal friends from those days often pop in and out of various mutual business endeavors. Also, as a venture capitalist, my value to the entrepreneurs we fund and the limited partners who entrust their money to us is maximized as we build our networks.

Much of our time at our firm is spent forging relationships with new, talented people and world-class research institutions. If you constantly add intelligent, successful people to your network, your performance as a venture capitalist is bound to improve. And time is on our side! As every year goes by, friends and colleagues tend to achieve new goals and get promoted to new positions of power and influence. It has been 17 years since I graduated from college, and I find it amazing to read of the interesting pursuits my former classmates are involved in. And shame on me if I don't make the effort to get in touch and stay in touch, to see if I can come up with something interesting to work on together.

It is very common for venture capitalists and the founders of a company to go out on social engagements before, during, and after the deal. Often family members are invited, and the line is certainly blurred between business and personal. We like to get to know everyone, and it is valuable to see people in different situations and realize they are in for the long run. It makes things a little more personal.

At a high level, the correct strategy going into a deal negotiation is to know everything about the technology of the new company, the potential markets for its products, and the people who are doing the negotiation. There is no excuse for being unprepared. Among other things, being prepared shows the entrepreneur the negotiation is entirely in good faith and that I want to put the deal together because I have passion for their idea and want to help make it a reality. After all, venture capitalists are ultimately service providers – we are here to help entrepreneurs realize their dreams. That is the driving force behind all successful venture capitalists. It is not a passion for making money; rather, it is a passion for helping entrepreneurs build great companies. Of course, if you help build many great companies, you will generate substantial financial returns for all parties involved, especially the limited partners of the venture capital fund. And thus the cycle can begin anew.

The system works only if substantial financial returns are generated; this allows limited partners to recycle some of those returns back into new funds, which allow new cash to be disbursed to deserving entrepreneurs. But if the focus is on making money and not building great companies, people will lose focus, and the cycle will break. I can not emphasize this point enough.

On the other hand, Wall Street folks are often transaction-focused. That works for them: Since they are in a different business, they have different goals, different responsibilities, different training, and different sources of capital. Early-stage venture capitalists are not transaction-focused. We are more like the entrepreneur. We get involved with the entrepreneur early on, and we want to help build a great company. Of course, good venture capitalists need to be very financially savvy and need to be experts at transactions because that is part of the job, but that usually isn't the main focus. In my ideal world, I strive to build and maintain a reputation and track record that would cause every entrepreneur, scientist, or engineer to want to work with me more than anyone else in the world.

You need to prove yourself constantly in this business and earn the right to work side-by-side with the world's best entrepreneurs. At our firm, we serve on the boards of all of our investments, and that is not a responsibility we take lightly. Every day we wake up and view the day as a another chance to excel. The focus is always on building great companies and doing whatever it takes to facilitate that.

At the beginning of the deal structuring and the negotiation process, it is important to be prepared and have your homework completed. Otherwise, the entrepreneur may view you, at best, as just a source of money, or at worst, the entrepreneur may decide to take money from another source because you haven't demonstrated your worth.

There are many ways to do your homework, including spending a lot of time with the entrepreneur, understanding what they do, having many lunches and dinners, meeting their family, having them meet your family, and having them meet all of my partners. I don't try to impress them, but I let them know I understand their area, and I emphasize relevant past experiences. This way, when it comes time for the actual negotiation, its main focus is not simply to paper over the transaction with help from some attorneys, but rather to complete the transaction and get on with the business of building the company.

You should never take for granted nor ever take lightly the dreams of entrepreneurs, because their ideas are often what they are devoting their lives to. Therefore, while the consummation of the transaction itself is a significant milestone, and should be celebrated as such, the real fun and challenge comes in executing on the business plan and building a great company. That is my deal making strategy: I go into it in such a way that the entrepreneur or scientist does not even feel it's a transaction, that it's more of a milestone along the way to building a great company.

If you have been involved completely in the process leading up to the negotiations, you are already prepared for them. You should not have to stay up and "cram" the night before as if for an exam. But it is absolutely critical that before the negotiation you know how badly all parties want a deal, what the motivations are, and what the styles and personalities are. You need to know all the details about their business. You don't want to keep asking such questions as, "What are the financial projections for the third year?" You need to know the revenue projections because you have to be able to negotiate in real time. So if the entrepreneur says the valuation is too low, you need to be able to say something along the lines of, "Let's discuss this issue. Here's the way we looked at it, based on the following facts we have. Please let me know what you think....." Then a productive discussion can ensue, as opposed to your being unprepared to back up terms and conditions, in which case you will look foolish flipping through documents in real-time, trying to come up with an answer. You will not be thought highly of if you cannot keep most (all) of the facts in your head and if you cannot be smart and think in real time. Being smart and hard-working is the price of admission to sit at the entrepreneur's side, and they deserve no less.

Likewise, when it comes down to the legal structures and the detailed term sheets, you never want to say, "I don't know about that – we'll let the lawyers worry about it." Or "Let me call my lawyer, I'm not sure." You should know it; you should have all the facts in your head and be able to explain the minutiae. Of course, the lawyers will eventually have to review all final documents, but the point is that a venture capitalist must have a diverse skill set and be a jack-of-all-trades.

Negotiating a Deal

Plenty of textbooks have been written about specific negotiation strategies and tactics, and most business schools require some form of mock negotiation class before conferring an MBA degree. Although much of the information presented in those books and classes probably falls in the category of "common sense made difficult," it is useful to mention a few key points.

Ideally, you should understand the other parties in the negotiation as well as you understand yourself. More specifically, you should know exactly the goal of the negotiation. As simple as that sounds, it is the most important place to start. That may sound like common sense, but many people do not know what they want out of a negotiation when they go in.

The next step is to figure out how straightforward and honest you will be with the party you are negotiating with. Often it is a good negotiating technique to let the other party know exactly what you want. In some deals, though, that can weaken your position because you have put all your cards on the table. But I find in venture-capital negotiations that usually is the best strategy – to let the other party know what is important to you. If I am an entrepreneur, I might say, "What's really important to me in this deal is that my ownership percentage and equity is as high as it can be. I'm not so much worried about legal terms that will be triggered in a future potential negative scenario. I'm so confident about my future, I don't care about that. So I'm willing to give on those terms if we can agree on a higher initial valuation." That's a case where being honest and putting your cards on the table actually facilitates the negotiation; things move more quickly, and everyone can get what they want.

Unfortunately, it is not always so simple for both parties to find a win-win scenario. But in venture-capital negotiations, it is usually best to be as forthright as possible before and during the negotiations.

That strategy is not appropriate for all types of negotiations, such as purchasing a house or negotiating a weapons treaty. Other things to keep in mind during a negotiation are to have firm limits set on the transaction. Make sure you know beforehand your acceptable ranges regarding all of the terms under negotiation. Although this is a passion business, never fall in love with any particular deal to the point where you are tempted to close it on unreasonable terms.

Depending on market conditions, it can be partially true that the venture capital firm has the upper hand in a deal because they have the money. However, that is too simplistic an analysis. There is always competition for the best deals, technologies, and entrepreneurs.

Since we often help co-found the companies ourselves, in many ways we see both sides of the story. For entrepreneurs we don't know, the best way to leverage our position is by pointing to our experience. We tell anecdotes. The reality is that people learn better from stories, from data, and from history. We have been helping entrepreneurs realize their dreams for more than 15 years now. So we have plenty of tales to tell regarding successful startups. Entrepreneurs are more impressed by a track record of success than anything else.

Since our firm has helped co-found or invest in the founding rounds of more than 95 companies over a 15-year period, we have a large number of successful CEO and other entrepreneurial senior managers who have led our investments. These folks are always happy to talk on our behalf to prospective new companies. Likewise, we have a large network of other senior professionals (investment bankers, accountants, attorneys, consultants, Fortune 500 contacts, for example) resulting from our 15 years of taking companies from inception to IPO or strategic acquisition. Having these people around who will verify what you say and add more color is very helpful when necessary to "win" a deal.

Institutional experience is very helpful during negotiations. For instance, if a party in the negotiation declares, "I don't think this term is fair," we can literally go back to our database and say, "Here are the 95 companies we have started, and the 400 financing rounds we have been a part of, and X% of them had this feature." That does not mean that it is right for them, and we are always happy to discuss points and compromise; but our experience gives us a lot of credibility. The entrepreneur does not think we are making it up as we go long. If you are a newer fund, you do not have those stories, and you cannot be authoritative in presenting that data. You do not even have the data there.

In early-stage venture-capital deals, what makes deals break down is lack of trust, period. In other types of transactions, trust is not necessary, such as arms control negotiations or some types of corporate M&A activity. Often no one trusts anyone in those cases, yet deals are still struck. However, in venture-capital relations, once trust is lost, deals are rarely completed. Everything else you can solve – even unrealistic expectations. That's a common one, where either the venture capitalist or the entrepreneur has an unrealistic expectation on the valuation. Sometimes they are miles apart, but you can solve that. But you can't resolve lack of trust. It gets back to the marriage analogy. Do you want to spend three to seven years with someone you don't even trust at the beginning? There will be plenty of time to get into arguments later.

An important thing to remember during the actual negotiations is that early-stage venture capital can often be an inherently homerun or strikeout business. If the company is a homerun, it can be a billion-dollar IPO in the future, and everyone is happy. If it is a strikeout, everyone can lose a majority of their money and time. In either case, it really doesn't matter what the exact valuation terms were during the original negotiation when the company was founded. So it's not prudent to burn up good will at the beginning of the relationship by arguing for the last dollar. In fact, a venture capitalist can help maximize the probability of building a billion-dollar company by taking the long-term view and ensuring that all parties feel happy after the negotiation. Part of that process is having a good relationship with the entrepreneur, and if you have to give a little bit on terms, it is more than worth it.

There are also many singles and doubles in the venture-capital business, and in these cases the finer points of the deal terms often wind up having more impact. So I'm not saying to give on all details; rather, keep in mind that the venture capital business is a risk-capital industry, so make sure you are always concentrating on the potential for big successes and companies that can change the world.

Building trust during a negotiation period is accomplished in many ways. Besides telling anecdotes and getting validation from third parties, a lot of trust is built (or lost) during the process leading up to the negotiations. Little things can make a big difference, and a series of little things are interpreted as a pattern of behavior. If you tell the entrepreneur you are going to come by his or her laboratory at 3 p.m., make sure you are there promptly. Such details are cumulative. If you say you are going to return a call the next day with a reference, do it, and do it early in the day. During the negotiations, make sure you approach them in the same way every hour and every day that the negotiations are going on. In some deals some individuals exhibit personality changes, where perhaps a good dinner was enjoyed the night before, and you thought you were close, and everybody was congenial. But the next morning, the person is glaring at you from across the table. In this case, the other party is playing games, using a common negotiating tactic. That tactic is a prescription for disaster in the venture-capital business, so it is best to avoid it. If you start out negotiations in a professional tone, do your best to keep them professional; otherwise, trust gets broken because the other party thinks you are insincere.

When we are negotiating at this stage, we are negotiating with some of the smartest, most accomplished scientists and entrepreneurs in the world. Do not play games with them because they will see through you. Even if you manage to fool someone, it does no good. As has been repeatedly emphasized, the goal of all venture-capital deals is to create great companies over the long term.

Once you are actually negotiating, track record is key in managing risk. If the entrepreneur has done it before, things are likely to go more smoothly, both during the negotiations and in the ensuing execution of the business plan. It is important for all sides to manage the process of negotiating as they would manage the company. Bad leaders and managers are bad in general – so if the negotiations go poorly, chances are the company will be unsuccessful, anyway.

We normally divide risk into three areas: people risk, market risk, and technology risk. People risk: Have they done this before? We do a lot of due diligence on people. We will call their third-grade teacher, if appropriate. Market risk: Do we think people are willing to buy this product now or in the future? Technology risk: Do we really think they can build this product? We look at those three dimensions continuously before, during, and after the deal. That is the framework we use. And you need to know when you're going to walk away on all three of those dimensions.

It is difficult for a venture fund to know when to walk away because a venture fund is inherently diversified. A fund may have 20 or more companies in any particular fund, and one or two huge hits can really make the fund. So you can afford to take some risks and gambles because that is what this business is about. If you are not taking enough gambles, you are not doing your job correctly. But how do you know when to walk away? You never really know *a priori,* but you have to know at your fund which of those three risks you are most comfortable with.

At our firm, we are very comfortable with people risk because we have worked with many people and have a large network. You can always help the entrepreneurs improve, and if they do not improve, often you can recruit other people to manage the company. We are comfortable with technology risks because we are a technology-focused firm. We have seen different technologies go in and out of fashion, and we have seen technology twist in the wind and then all of a sudden solidify into something meaningful. So you have to understand the technology deeply not to be affected by short-term exuberance or panic in the market.

Market risk is a little harder for us. If somebody comes to us with a new idea and says: "Trust me, in two years everyone will be buying Scotch tape on the World Wide Web, so you need to fund me, and my business is Scotchtape.com." We are not comfortable with that, because who knows if people are going to start changing their behavior? But if a business comes to me with a new semiconductor circuit that can reduce costs by a factor of 100 and reduce power consumption by a factor of 100, I do not even need to think about the market. If you have a patent-protected technological breakthrough that enables a unique, useful product, the market is often there. That can be verified quickly by talking to a few customers, as opposed to scotchtape.com, which requires some hypothetical mass change in human behavior.

Success to me in a deal is not measured until years after the deal. You just do not know how to measure it. As Steve Jobs from Apple once said, "A transaction is a success if it enables the continuing growth of the company." A company is successful long-term if they make products and or services that customers want and will pay for. Eventually that translates into an IPO or a very nice acquisition, which can be considered success. In the end, success is defined by money, because that is how our system works.

So how do I view a successful transaction? In the long-term, seven years down the road, I will tell you if it was successful or not, because by then I will know if you have built great products and built a great company, and money will flow to all those who risked their money seven years earlier. In the short term, how can one measure success in a negotiation? I would ask in response, "Have we created or preserved a climate where we can continue to work together and respect one another as we journey down this road of building a great company?" The answer to that comes down to everybody feeling they were treated fairly. If anyone comes away from that transaction thinking they were unfairly taken advantage of, then it was a failure, even if in the short term you look like a hero because you got some esoteric legal term in the contract that you think is going to benefit you later.

Succeeding in Deal Making as an Individual

Venture capital is a long-term business. I am 38 years old now; I love working and plan to be in this business for another 20 or 30 years. So in the short term, if I lose a deal because I am very honest and straightforward, then that is OK. In the long run it is more important to earn a reputation as someone with integrity who follows through on his commitments. Although that may sound altruistic, it is actually the best way to ensure that our firm has great companies in our portfolio. The only thing you have in this business is your reputation. It takes years to build a reputation as a great venture capitalist, but it can be lost very quickly if you don't conduct yourself with integrity. In other fields that are defined only by this year's bonus pool, talk of integrity may make some people snicker. But in venture capital, I know that if I am helpful to someone, it will benefit me in the long run – not to mention that being helpful to others is its own reward. Of course, our limited partners are not entrusting their money to us just so we can go around being nice to others. They want us to be effective, and that means generating superior financial returns over the long term. As I've mentioned, there are many aspects of generating superior financial returns, and in isolation, an individual aspect may not appear to contribute to superior returns. That is the art of the deal: recognizing pieces of a puzzle that individually appear to be useless or meaningless, yet when assembled properly, yield a surprising and useful result.

The legends in the venture capital industry are usually described as individuals of great integrity. Sure, they often have strong personalities, and they do what needs to be done, but being honest and respected is not incongruous with being financially successful.

In summation, to succeed in the venture capital profession, you have to be passionate. Mountaineers have a saying that sounds rather trite, but actually speaks volumes: Before you can consider yourself a mountaineer, you have to spend your time in the mountains. There is no substitute for going out and doing something – doing lots of deals, helping build great companies, working seven days a week, talking to lots of people, and loving it. If you do not love it, it is going to show. It is like being an artist: You would do it even if you were not getting paid any money. It's true, the most famous VCs, even though they are wealthy, would be VCs even if they weren't getting paid.

I love this stuff, and you can tell I love this stuff. So to me that is how you keep your edge – just keep loving it. Once you stop loving it, you will lose your edge; you will become less successful; and you should find something else to do. There is a lot you can do in this world. You do not have to be an entrepreneur, and you do not have to be a venture capitalist.

Patrick Ennis is a partner with ARCH Venture Partners. ARCH has been investing in seed- and early-stage technology companies for more than 15 years and has special expertise in building technology companies with leading academics and entrepreneurs. ARCH manages more than $700 million in capital, and operates nationally *with offices in Albuquerque, Austin, Chicago, New York, and Seattle.*

Dr. Ennis is based in Seattle and concentrates primarily in information technology and physical sciences, including communications, optics, semiconductors, and medical imaging. He has helped organize a number of companies within these disciplines and serves on the boards of directors of Impinj, Advanced Diagnostics, MidStream Technologies, and LightCross, and is a board observer for Malibu Networks, Quarry Technologies, Nanosys, and Xtera Communications.

Before joining ARCH in 1998, Dr. Ennis held several senior positions with Lucent Technologies, AT&T, and Bell Labs. These included lead roles in Product Management for Optical Networking and Switching devices, Consumer Marketing, where he led three new product launches and major advertising campaigns, and Software Engineering where he led projects in speech recognition, network design, and competitive local service.

Before joining Bell Labs in 1991, Dr. Ennis conducted research in nuclear physics at several national laboratories in the U.S., Canada, and England. He discovered new energy states of rare isotopes of Germanium and published 15 articles describing his work.

Dr. Ennis holds an MBA from the Wharton School of Business, a Ph.D. in physics from Yale University, and a BS in mathematics and physics from the College of William and Mary, where he was elected Phi Beta Kappa.

COMMUNICATING WITH CLIENTS: BRIDGING THE TRANSLATION GAP

GERARD S. DIFIORE

Reed Smith

Corporate & Securities Group Head

Educating the Client

One of the most challenging parts of doing deals is dealing with the entrepreneurial client who does not understand the process of deal making. You have to educate that client and be a translator of the process, so the client can understand what they are supposed to do. Entrepreneurs are experts in writing software, designing optical switches, or other innovations – that is what they know, their business, their point of reference. They are very smart people. But they don't understand there is a business to deal making. And they don't always realize that that business of deal making is something the lawyer knows, or that the investment banker knows, but that they don't know. And they don't always take the process cues that they ought to be taking to allow the deal to happen in the most favorable way.

Communication problems are common. The lawyer talks to the client; the client talks to the other client; that client talks to their lawyer, and then it goes back through the other way. What an inefficient expenditure of time and energy! It is usually much more effective to get everyone locked in a meeting room and to hammer the issues out in a two- or three-day session, where the clients say: "Here is the scope of the things we agree upon as business people. Let's write them on a piece of paper, put a box around them, get the hell out of the room, and let the lawyers finish the job."

It also helps if the fine-point negotiating happens with only the lawyers after the business people have shaken hands on the big-picture items. There are several benefits to this. First, the relationship-building process between the business people is not damaged, and second, it usually takes much less time. It is all about deal momentum. Since the parties are going to have to live with each other going forward, it is much better for the lawyers to fight about the details. I find that process problems are far more prevalent when the people you are across from or alongside are not people who do deals for a living. That is one of the most challenging things about deal making in the entrepreneurial environment.

I have a list of business books that I recommend to people. I either give them the list or give them the books. Many clients are willing to be self-starters and invest a little time in educating themselves. I use the books especially when I have clients with intellectual property and human capital as key aspects of their businesses, and they are not sure what to do with it or how to protect it or build companies around it. I also give them books that relate to the corporate finance process, the capital raising process, the M&A process. I find that if they are willing to read a couple of those books and learn the language, they are much better able to follow the cues that come during the deal process. That gives the process a much higher likelihood of success. It is also much more rewarding because they can better appreciate the value you bring to the deal process.

Valuation Stubbornness and Other Challenges

Another challenge is trying to explain market dynamics to a client who thinks the pricing or valuation terms of their deal deviate materially from their own expectations, up or down. Sometimes you have an early-stage company raising money in a Series A transaction, and management is insistent in its view that the company is worth X, but everybody is coming to them and saying, "The company is worth X minus 40 percent." Many times they do not understand that if nobody is willing to pay X, then at that moment in time, the company is simply not worth X, since no one will pay that price or place that value on it. This is an especially trying problem in volatile markets or markets where certain industries come in and out of favor. While it may be considered harsh, in the long run management occasionally needs to be told to take a "reality pill" and accept a different valuation if they want some chance to get a deal accomplished. Numerous deal structures can be fashioned to bridge this valuation gap, with retrospective adjustments as a means of splitting the difference, so to speak. But these mechanisms can never achieve their purpose if the parties cannot agree to a basic price to start from.

Obviously, for clients not accustomed to complex transaction structures, it can all seem very intimidating. In fact, even things that are routine for the deal lawyers can be intimidating to entrepreneurial clients who are experts in their own universe, but not experts in deals. Rather than needlessly confuse them with details, the best thing to do is get your proposal in front of them, so they have a reference point, rather than just talking endlessly about where you want to go and what you want to do. Discussion is useful to plant the basic seeds in their minds, but then you have to put something tangible in front of them that they can use as a reference point. Then you can talk off that and refine the proposal to get where you need to go. It is much better and more time efficient to stick with the important business issues, especially if you have a client who is entrepreneurial and not just a business development person.

In my practice I have two universes of clients. I work with a lot of early-stage companies, entrepreneurial types who have a technical background and who are not MBAs or business development officers by trade. Those people need a special kind of guidance to effectively corral their skills and attention in the right direction. If you give them something to work from, and discuss a piece of paper that is in front of them, you are much better off. For example, I have a client that is a services-based software development company and they are interested in buying a services division from a public company. That public company also makes software products but is trying to get into the software customization business on the side. The client, an IT person, is very technology-literate, but not business- or finance-literate. He told me what he thought he wanted to accomplish in the deal. But then as the discussion continued, I asked him: "Do you want to assume liabilities or not?" And he was immediately lost in the discussion.

So instead you put in front of him a letter of intent, and then you go over it with him, work your way down the items on the list and ask: "What do you think about this? What do you think about that?" That focuses him on what he needs to worry about, and then you have real feedback on the key issues, so you can get something out the door that is meaningful to advance the process.

Managing Expectations and Understanding the Process

It is very hard to explain to entrepreneurs that negotiating is nothing personal, just business. Entrepreneurs are, after all, people, people who have started companies. They take such ownership in everything they create that they are sometimes unwilling or unable to dissociate themselves from the hurt or the disappointment when the other side in a deal is not seeing things the way they see them. If this disparity cannot be overcome, it is impossible for the entrepreneur to consummate the transaction. I have seen companies fail because of the entrepreneur's unwillingness to accept a valuation that is lower than they think it should be. It is like the man who has five offers on his house, but none matches his asking price, so he never sells the house!

This problem will probably get worse before it gets better, especially in today's environment where, at least as far as I've seen, valuations continue to decline, and depending on what crystal ball you are reading about what will happen with the economy going forward, there may be further declines in valuations across the board. You have to manage expectations. Sometimes the expectations you try to manage are those of the client vis-à-vis the other side; sometimes the expectations you try to manage are between you and the client.

One company I am currently working with provides an example of the communication challenges you typically face in doing deals for emerging companies. It is a great company, in the early stage of development, with an innovative health care diagnostic device. They have developed a truly terrific and useful product and received recognition from trade fairs. They have great technology that they acquired from a world-class research university, and have made many modifications and improvements to the technology to make it a useful device. They have a high-quality management team that is going out to try to raise more money to execute on a sound business plan. Sounds like a Cinderella story.

We have been helping them obtain patents, and we and their other advisors have been introducing them to venture capitalists and other private-equity financing sources. But it has been very frustrating because the management team does not understand the VC investment process or what a typical deal timeline is actually like. Understandably, management is very focused on product development refinements and addressing manufacturing, marketing, and other operational issues relating to implementing the business plan once the funding is in place. These are all certainly critical management tasks and are precisely the things VCs evaluate when considering making their investments. Without unrelenting progress on these fronts, the prospects of the business could be impaired, and I am not suggesting these items be ignored.

But management did not always understand that the "business of raising money is a business unto itself." It, too, requires sustained attention and energy from management to make the process moves ahead, just like the attention and energy being devoted to the company's core business – a second, but simultaneous, full-time job, so to speak, and not the same as a "night job," I might add. This means that when people make introductions to investors who ask for information, the company needs to get it to them. You have to follow up right away; you have to make sure it is what they need; and you can't just call back the next week. In the highly competitive environment of raising early-stage capital, responsiveness and tenacity are key factors in how management's success potential is evaluated by investors, and perceptions mean a lot.

While the company did get funded, the process was delayed. Not only is time money, but delays in volatile markets can have an immense impact on enterprise value. There are good arguments on the other side, of course, for example, that the additional time enabled management to increase enterprise value, and the company was able to move its plan forward. But that can be a risky way to play when the company is burning cash, and the tank is nearly empty. Had management failed to focus ultimately on the investment process, the result could have been different. Had they said, "We'll get to that, we'll get to that," by the time they did get to it, they might not have had a company.

Execution Issues

It is strange, but in my experience I have found there is no relationship between the quality of the idea or product and the ability of the entrepreneurial team to quickly master the investment process to maximize the chance for rapid funding, in the short run, and thereby maximize enterprise success in the long run. I have never been able to figure that out, and it's probably one of my biggest personal frustrations.

This problem can be acute, especially when it involves entrepreneurs who have never been involved in financing an emerging company. In my other example, the product is a winner: It is something that is good for the world and good for business, and it will do good things for society. It is a winning idea and a winning product. In terms of actually being able to run the business going forward, the management team is a winning team. But in terms of quickly learning the process of what needed to be done to get the business funded at this stage of the game, I think there was a disconnect.

Understanding Client Needs

When I am approaching a deal and looking at all the moving parts, I try my best to understand my client's objective, and I ask myself: "What do they think they really need?" And then I ask: "What does my experience tell me they really need?" Those two things are often not the same, unless I am dealing with a very experienced client who has been down that particular path before. If it is an entrepreneurial client, those universes may overlap, but rarely do they completely intersect.

I try to make sure I educate the client and give them the benefit of all of my vicarious experience. In many ways – and this is why deal lawyers often end up on the business side after years and years of doing deals – many deal lawyers feel they are much better at this game than their clients, even at making business decisions. They would probably not admit to that, but it is often true. So the goal is to try to transfer the knowledge and the experience you have to the client, so the client comes away with that higher level of understanding. That is very gratifying. If the client gets that education, it creates a great bond of loyalty. Some people might say, "If you do that, you may reduce dependency because you're not the expert anymore." That's the wrong way to look at it. In my view, anyone who looks at it that way is shortsighted and is missing the boat. The best lawyers are those who empower their clients.

It is a great thing when a client comes to you and says, "Not only did you do the deal for me, and that was great, but you also educated me in the process of doing deals." That education you give the client is something they appreciate because they view it as a bonus over and above what they expected. That also builds personal relationships, and that's part of the payback to me. Getting the paycheck is great – no qualms there. But the real payback is the relationships I've built, the friendships I've created, and probably most importantly, the knowledge that companies I have worked with have done good things and made products that benefit the world.

Succeeding in Deal Making as an Individual

Successful deal makers have four key characteristics. These are in no particular order:

❑ You have to be a good listener. You have to listen carefully to not only what is said, but also what is meant, and understand the real message.

❑ You have to maintain a sense of creativity and adaptability to be a good deal maker because directions often change. Things move around in a deal; nothing stands still.

❑ To be a great deal maker, you need to be able to focus at more than one level. You need to be able to focus at the macro level of the issues, and you also need to make sure the right people focus on the micro level of specifics that may also be important. The devil is in the details.

❑ The final element of successful deal making is having the energy and the persistence to create and maintain deal momentum. You have to be highly energetic; you have to be a fast study; and you have to be adaptable. You have to be able to take something you have done for somebody else and mold it into something that works for your current situation without reinventing the wheel.

In my opinion, from a lawyer's perspective, what separates the really great deal makers from the average ones is precision. Precision is critical. Precision in drafting a letter of intent and precision in defining things can make a huge difference down the road when you are fighting over something, or when a court or arbitrator is looking at an agreement, trying to figure out what was meant or what the parties agreed to. It takes only a little more energy, and a lot more focus, to be precise or unambiguous.

A major flaw I see in many deal lawyers is sloppiness. Sloppiness breeds ambiguity, and ambiguity can create problems in the future. Some people would argue that some ambiguity is intentional, or that there can be benefits to ambiguity in agreements or in deals. There are times when that is probably true. But as a general rule, ambiguity does not work to your advantage if you really know what you are doing when crafting agreements. That is another of the things that separate a good deal maker from a really great one, elevating the practice to an art.

This may not be something a non-lawyer can readily appreciate, but with a great deal maker, the papers will have elegance. That is becoming a lost art in this business, and I hate to say that, but I still appreciate elegance in drafting.

Another thing that separates a good deal maker from a great one is understanding when to stop negotiating. A person may be trying so hard to do a great job that he or she doesn't realize the additional things they are doing are no longer adding value. That is a very transaction-specific kind of thing; but I think a great negotiator can get something done in two rounds that an average one might get done in five. So being thoughtful, thorough, and complete – and knowing when to stop – separate the good deal lawyers from the great deal lawyers. If you want to sum that up in just one word, it is simple: perspective.

Finally there is the whole issue of passion. It is very important to be passionate about what you do. If you can't do it with passion, then, do something else. I am really lucky to be passionate about what I do because this game is too exhausting, too hard, and too depressing if you don't have passion. It will eat you up.

Negotiation Strategy

First of all, you must truly understand the client's goal in the transaction and get as close as possible to having that goal realized. People engaged in a deal recognize that many deals will not be successful, so whether the deal closes may or may not define success for them. The transaction itself may not be the ultimate goal; it may be the means to something else. So you need to be mindful of the client's goal in the transaction and to get them as close to it as possible.

Of course, the goal will vary with each deal. You may have circumstances where people will pursue transactions to get close to other companies, and find out that they really don't want the M&A transaction they thought they wanted once they looked at the business and saw what there was to see; instead, they change their focus and do a strategic transaction that does not really buy or sell anything. I have seen this happen often in the services and software sectors, where the proposed M&A transaction is how the parties get to know one another better, but at the end of the day, they realize a transaction would not be good for either of them.

If you have pursued the first transaction in a way that does not destroy either side's ego and keeps people open-minded about getting something done, you have the opportunity to do the second deal. However, if you do the first piece too aggressively, so one side or the other gets alienated, then neither side has the chance to pursue the second piece. I view that as a failure. You cannot always have the business people know in the beginning whether they want that strategic relationship, as opposed to something else. They are not always sure. So you take a slightly circuitous route to get to the ultimate goal, and if, in the process, you have been too aggressive or have alienated the businesspeople, you cannot say you have done a successful deal.

One of the most important strategies is not to negotiate against yourself. When doing a deal, I always build in giveaways, or "give-ups." If you have 14 open points on which there is no agreement, the client may really only need four of those to be satisfied, and they don't care about the rest. So I might have the client add on a couple of other points that are giveaways. That way, when they go back to the other side, they have room to negotiate. Unless you build those things in, you are negotiating against yourself and leaving no negotiating room. A giveaway is a buffer. It creates an opportunity for your adversary to feel he came away from the table with something. Maybe he did, and maybe he didn't. This is a lot easier to do when you represent the party with more of the overall transaction leverage.

It's also important to understand which part of something is valuable to the other party. The part you think is valuable may not always be the part the other party needs. Think about this in terms of an orange: Somebody might want the juice; somebody might want the seeds; somebody might want the skin; and somebody might want the rind – and each part may be very useful to each person. As an intelligent negotiator, be mindful that you may be able to give up parts that would be useful to the other side. Sometimes when you can do that, you have a better chance of reaching agreement. You have to think about all of the parts at stake to figure out the best way to get what everyone wants.

Having the Guts to Walk Away

Most people do not have the guts to walk away from a deal. And most do not know how to be a gutsy negotiator in a polite, businesslike manner. You do not have to be a nasty, disgusting person to be a forthright, forceful, aggressive negotiator. And most clients do not recognize the power of being able to walk away. I think I try to instill that in clients but am not as successful as I would like. I say, don't always look at what you give up if you don't do the deal – look at what you give up if you do do the deal. It all has to do with associations and whether people look at a transaction as a way of either avoiding pain or pursuing something good.

Most humans think and act in ways that guide them to avoid pain, but few think and act in ways to pursue pleasure. Let's take that into the client context. Once people have gone down the road to do a deal, they think the other side will get angry or upset, or their synergistic relationship with them will be destroyed, when they walk. They get locked into thinking that.

People have to remember the best loss may be their first loss. It is the same thing with an investor who invests in a company and then realizes it was a mistake. Now what do they do? Do they put more good money after bad, or do they say, "My best loss is my first loss." The smart investors in my view take the latter approach. If you have made a mistake, it's a mistake. If you can't fix it, don't try. Have the power to walk away. I think nowadays that is a tough thing, when people have so many portfolio companies they are trying to nurse along, and investors have become so gun-shy that they do not want to pull the trigger on anything new.

But I have been involved in situations where investors – the ones I think are the smartest ones – say to themselves, "You know what? This was a mistake. Let's get over it. We're not perfect. Let's take the ego out of it and make the smart choice, which is to do nothing more." I have seen many deals consummated that were actually failures because clients didn't have the guts to walk away before the deal was done, because they had taken too much ownership in the process. They failed to realize they had lost all perspective, and that the deal that they wanted in the beginning is not what they got at the end of the day.

These things don't fail on day one, but later. Many are catastrophic failures that tragically ruin lives. Doing a deal is like getting married. Going into it, you think the person walking down the aisle is the love of your life; but when you look across and are about to exchange vows, you pause and think, "Wait a minute! That's not the person I thought it was, it's somebody else." You are at the altar; all the witnesses are there; the families are there; and you think, "This is the wrong thing to do." It is difficult to walk away.

It is the same with deals. When you are in a deal, you have all the professionals, the business people, and the bankers around you, and there is a certain level of ceremony to all of it. You still need to be able to gracefully say, "This isn't the right thing, and these are the reasons. I want to shake hands and go away friends, but we're not doing this deal."

Deal Momentum

You often start out with a frantic call from someone because either they got a letter of intent, or they want to do a letter of intent. Suddenly, you're in a frenzy for the next day or two, or maybe even in a half-day or few hours, you spit out that letter of intent and send it to the other side. That is just the beginning. You need to be able to maintain that level of momentum and keep everybody involved and on the same path to have a shot at getting the deal where it needs to go.

Many clients don't have the time, the energy, or the depth of resources to devote people on their staff to getting that done. I am from the school that says the lawyer has to be willing to take charge. That is probably truer for entrepreneurial transactions for emerging growth companies than when you are doing a transaction for a Fortune 100 company that has a zillion people on its staff. But since I am heavily focused on emerging, entrepreneurial companies, I teach my associates: You're the boss; you take control; you're the focal point; you make it happen. That's usually because the clients have so many other distractions distracting them from keeping their foot on the gas, that it really becomes the lawyer's job to run the deal. It will be very clear to you when your client doesn't want that. They will tell you, "I am the businessperson; you're not. I'll make the decisions; I'll set the agenda."

But many clients are very happy to be relieved of the control position because it is not their business. Their business is making products, writing software, building networks, designing optical switches, whatever. They don't know how to get the deal done. In my experience, it is actually better when clients relinquish that seat and let the lawyer run the deal.

You have to create deal momentum. If you can't create momentum, you will never get the deal done. And I think the momentum isn't always self-sustaining; it just isn't always going to be there. So you need to find ways to keep the momentum in the deal long enough, at least, for the deal to get to the point where people feel they are in too far to turn back. You have to be willing to take an aggressive leadership role; it is part of running the deal and making the deal happen. Deals don't happen by themselves. They happen because people make them happen.

Gerard S. DiFiore joined Reed Smith in 1997. He is a member of the firm's Business and Finance Department and chairman of its Securities Review Committee. Mr. DiFiore's practice is concentrated in the representation of clients involved in sophisticated securities and corporate transactional matters.

Mr. DiFiore's clients, many of whom are in the technology field, range from entrepreneurial, early-stage enterprises to publicly traded companies. Mr. DiFiore is experienced in assisting clients in all stages of the corporate growth cycle. On the financing source side, he represents underwriters and placement agents, investment and commercial banks, and other private equity sources.

Mr. DiFiore frequently represents issuers and underwriters in securities offerings and similar corporate finance activities. Typical transactions include venture-capital financings (preferred stock or convertible debt, with warrants); private placements and bridge financings (debt, equity, and combinations); public offerings (IPOs, resale registrations, and secondaries); mergers and acquisitions; exchange offers; joint-venture formations; spin-offs; special dividends; and recapitalizations, reorganizations, commercial lending, and other bank-related transactions, workouts, and buyouts.

Mr. DiFiore advises public companies on SEC periodic reporting and proxy requirements and counsels management on routine compliance issues, such as Section 16 reporting (short swing profits), Rule 144 sales, and Williams Act matters. He also represents registered broker-dealers, investment companies, and investment advisors on matters and transactions arising under federal and state securities laws. In addition to representing clients in capital-raising activities, Mr. DiFiore regularly negotiates a wide range of commercial arrangements, such as distribution, consulting, licensing, trademark, shareholder, operating, partnership, confidentiality, and employment agreements.

Mr. DiFiore has been engaged in the private practice of securities and corporate law for more than ten years, following his service with the U.S. Securities and Exchange Commission in Washington, D.C., where he was ultimately named Counsel to the SEC's EDGAR Rulemaking Taskforce.

Mr. DiFiore received his BA in economics, with honors, from the University of Vermont in 1981 and received his JD, cum laude, from Suffolk University School of Law in 1984. Mr. DiFiore is admitted to practice in New York, New Jersey, and Massachusetts and is a member of the American Bar Association and the New Jersey State Bar Association. He serves on the ABA's Committee on Federal Regulation of Securities (including service on the Task Forces on Small Business Issuers and Electronic Communications) and the Securities Law Committee of the New Jersey Bar Association.

DEAL MAKING: THE INTERPERSONAL ASPECTS

JOHN M. ABRAHAM

Battery Ventures

Venture Partner

The Deal Maker

The art of deal making is akin to the act of transforming a partially molded block of clay into a work of fine art. Although many aspects of deal making, such as valuation or legal documentation, are more scientific than artistic, a good deal maker, like an artist, must have an unorthodox approach to problem-solving. In an artistic sense, the deal maker envisions the finished product and molds the transaction in a way that may not have been imagined before. Deal making involves a great deal of creativity, which is why formulaic, "cookie-cutter" deals are more like signing up a franchisee than creating a partnership.

Along with creativity, characteristics of a good deal maker include honesty, empathy, and a willingness to understand the other side's point of view. It is important to be knowledgeable about the market, and it helps to be articulate, energetic, and reasonably gregarious. A strong work ethic is essential; a good deal maker must be able to tolerate frustration and a roundabout approach to the goal.

In a pure sense, the best deal makers are those who are highly conversant with the content of what is being discussed, as opposed to those who simply steward the process. It is easy for people who aren't experienced at transactional business to make the mistake of always being in a selling mode. It is much more important to be a balanced listener and end up with a genuine understanding of what the other side is doing. You also need to understand the concepts and the level of performance a company relies upon. Command of detail makes the difference between a great and an average practitioner. In addition, the best deal makers keep their objectives in mind at all times. It's relatively easy to get carried away with the idea of getting the deal done at all costs. It's also fairly common for people in deal making situations to get emotional and to take things personally. But it's best to remember that all deals are done for business reasons, and that achieving a reasonable outcome requires great objectivity.

Like anything else, luck and timing should never be underestimated. These factors are as responsible for great deal makers as anything else.

Deal Making Strategies

A lot of preparation precedes any transaction. This preparation includes reading about the company wherever information is available and looking at other companies with similar characteristics. It is relatively easy to become well acquainted with almost every aspect of a company. A general level of preparedness involves a degree of comfort with the company's content area and nomenclature. You should be able to carry on a discussion in terms that are familiar to the other side.

At a more specific level, it is highly important to understand the capital structure of the company and to recognize where political sensitivities reside. Most venture deals have primary owners, and in situations involving private companies or closely held public companies, it is critical to keep these owners in mind, even if they are not members of the management team. Recognizing the needs of this constituency also helps determine what avenues might be possible and successful.

It is also important to recognize the commercially competitive aspects that exist around an investment to control the seller's inevitable sense of paranoia. Understanding the expectations of the other party will help you prepare a line of reasoning that will successfully address those expectations. A key element of any meaningful transaction, therefore, involves a willingness to engage in mutual, almost consultative, problem-solving with the other side. The simplest way to view this is to focus on the main motivation of the other side. For example, in a venture deal, it is nearly axiomatic that the company is seeking funding to "grow the business." However, if there are immediate cash pressures that confront the business, then it is often possible to structure a transaction that freezes out competition by agreeing to provide interim financing that serves as a bridge loan. In other transactions, such as mergers, the owners' driving motivations might be related to estate planning or other liquidity considerations. Even if the merger is structured as a stock-based deal, it is often advantageous to provide for cash liquidity, at least in part, for the primary owners. In competitive situations, these "extraordinary" considerations often make a huge difference in helping you win the deal.

In an ideal world, each side would have the other side's interests at heart. Empathy and mutual understanding are often prevented, however, by a discrepancy in the levels of experience at the table. For example, a large company in the process of acquiring a smaller company usually possesses a greater level of sophistication. In a corporate context, the larger company usually has a broader agenda, and the acquisition serves a predetermined purpose, such as product enhancement or entrance into a new market. Because the smaller company's perspective is narrower, it tends to be overly protective of its resources and unrealistic in its expectations. The only way to solve this problem is to bring the levels of understanding to parity.

A dimension of parity and trust can be forged between the two sides by an almost excessive display of candor; in essence, it is necessary to "show the cards before the game is played." The most important tools that a deal maker brings to the table are candor and absolute integrity. One way to employ this crucial set of ethical principles is to expose yourself in ways that people might think are inimical to your interests, but that actually serve you very well in the long run.

For example, rather than being perceived as having exacted the last measure of value in a deal, it is more effective to be seen as having given more than was necessary. This strategy not only has the potential to bind you to the other side, but also provides you with the "moral high ground." By taking this high ground, you will not have to suffer any pangs of guilt later, nor will you have to apologize later for demanding a consistency of performance. In a certain situation, for instance, it might be advantageous to pay more for a company than you think it is worth because you can then hold the company to a higher standard than you might be able to if you hadn't extended yourself by paying a premium.

Another important strategy in deal making is availability. Be sure, always, to provide people with the resources they need to answer any questions they might have. Take this principle to a precise, almost surgical, step-by-step level to ensure the other side understands exactly what will take place in a deal. Although it may sound trite, it is very important to meticulously deliver on the promises you make with respect to the tasks and the timing associated with completing a deal. If you manage to do this, you will easily differentiate yourself from others who are more casual in their approach to completing a transaction. It may seem simplistic, but sellers "project" reliability in the process into a belief that this reliability "signals" that you are also willing and able to close the deal.

The key issue here is in keeping with the theme of this chapter, namely, that mutual trust governs all great transactions. Buyers and sellers both must realize the true acknowledgement between parties takes place before the legal documents are drafted. An agreement exists when both sides look one another in the eye, shake hands, and agree on the next steps.

The (Gentle) Art of Persuasion

In a venture-capital context, most opportunities have leverage built into them: 1) The company needs money. 2) The company needs money quickly. In these cases it is not necessary to exert leverage that does not already exist in the situation. In an M&A setting, it is much easier to get excited about using leverage. After all, one organization is usually doing the buying, and the other is doing the selling. It's always tempting to use position to try to gain an advantage, but it's even more effective to put yourself into the other person's shoes.

The easiest, cleanest and quickest way to be persuasive is to articulate your standards up front. If these standards are rejected, then you must determine whether you want to go forward. For example, if you are willing to pay only a certain price, or to use a particular security, it's best to state that position firmly at the beginning of a negotiation. This helps you establish credibility with the other side. They might think you are just "role playing" with them, and they will often offer an alternative. If this counter-offer runs contrary to your standards, then you are able to further demonstrate credibility by walking away from the deal.

It's interesting to remember that some of the best deals ever recorded are the ones that never got done. If you relax your standards without a terribly good reason, you are destined to sponsor regretful transactions.

Today (and in most market conditions), venture-capital firms basically can choose the deals they wish to make, and, at the end of the day, they can always walk away from deals that have onerous terms. On the other side of the table, companies operating with a level of consistency and integrity will clearly telegraph what they are willing to tolerate. In theory, then, it ought to be quite easy for "standard" venture deals to be negotiated. But in practice, it is far more challenging to consummate these transactions. One interesting situation arises with respect to the security most venture capital companies use. The "standard" security venture-capital firms use is called participating preferred convertible stock. Despite that a participating preferred security is a standard that venture-capital firms are usually unwilling to forego, there is much late-stage discussion about this particular deal term. If both sides were candid about their objectives at the outset, then a fundamental term like this particular security would be discussed much earlier in the process.

Persuading the other side should not be difficult if each side is willing to listen. If a deal starts to feel uncomfortable or too hard to manage, then you shouldn't go through with it. There is no transaction you cannot live without. As you move further into the process, you should recognize that you are being educated about a number of things – the people, the legal environment, the process itself – in ways you never could have imagined. If the deal doesn't get easier as time passes, then you might be violating your original objectives. People tend to want to complete things they start, and they try to let the momentum of the project take over. Good deal making requires the objectivity and discipline to constantly check progress against goals. From the deal maker's perspective, you should be prepared to make your best offer, to extend yourself to get the tasks done, and to defend what you are proposing to all involved on the buying side of the transaction.

Sellers, on the other hand, should consider the following: If you're not willing to sell an asset for $X, then that is the price at which you just bought it. Sellers need to evaluate whether they would be willing to repurchase their business for the price being offered. Sellers (or those who receive significant venture financing) need to be equally critical with respect to their objectives. If the financing or the buyout doesn't significantly enhance your net worth, then you should seriously evaluate your motivation.

Defining Success

Many people genuinely believe their job is to exact every last dollar from a deal or transaction. Others believe they are successful only when they achieve the "best" terms. Because deal making involves people as well as assets, these approaches are shortsighted. In a successful deal, people are happy in their working environment long after the deal has been made. The tangibles and intangibles of the business have been understood, so that those people who wanted to leave were given the first opportunity to do so, and those who wanted to stay were given the resources and assistance necessary to build a strong business.

These achievements can be quantified only in hindsight. If, after three of four years have passed, it is possible to say the company is functioning within a tolerance of success predicted at the outset, then the deal is a success. On an emotional level, a successful deal instills a sense of pride.

The Future of Deal making

In terms of corporate deal making, the future will bring a trend toward transactions that involve cash. If the markets stay turbulent, there will be a flight from stock transactions. After all, who enjoys the prospect of trading your life's work for the "good feeling" that comes from the transitory "win" in a merger where the acquiring company's stock subsequently crashes?

In the venture realms, there will be a flight to quality, which means venture firms will be extraordinarily selective, and the terms negotiated will be more exacting. Deal makers will accentuate the importance of the value-added, whether this takes the form of additional services, consultative advice, or knowledge of the market.

Corporate and venture deals will continue to flourish in the present economy and in the next. The reason for this is fundamental: People have an inveterate need to cooperate. Venture capital and corporate M&A serve a very real purpose in both the business and the psychological contexts.

Since 1986, John M. Abraham has worked closely with Battery Ventures on a number of joint investments, including Business Software Technology (now part of Computer Associates), Witness Systems (NASDAQ: WITS), Corillian Corporation (NASDAQ: CORI), Altra Energy, and Excelergy. With more than 25 years of experience in high technology investing, executive management, and product development, Mr. Abraham has successfully fulfilled various functions including senior vice president-

Engineering at Boole & Babbage (now part of BMC Software), CEO at Condor Technology and Add-Vision, Inc., and executive vice president at Compuware (NASDAQ: CPWR).

As a venture partner at Battery, Mr. Abraham focuses his attention on investments in the software and e-Business sectors. He is a member of the boards of directors at Optiant, Inc., OpenCola, Inc., Crystallize, Inc., and ElementUSA. He was educated in computer science at Columbia University and the University of Illinois.

MAKING A DEAL WORK

KENNETH K. BEZOZO

Haynes and Boone

Partner and Section Chair, Business Transactions

Finding Ways to Make It Work

For an attorney, a significant deal making strength is the ability to understand the needs and goals of people. The attorney must be able to understand people from the initial meeting, to read who is motivated to complete a particular transaction and who is less motivated or even, perhaps, reluctant to do so. The attorney must identify the leverage points present with respect to the transaction, as well as who has the stronger and weaker positions relative to those points. In addition, the attorney must be able to identify and understand the most significant aspects of the deal from each party's perspective, and how those aspects will affect the parties and the potential transaction.

Certainly, intelligence and intuition are very important characteristics of an effective deal maker. To be successful, an attorney must have a comprehensive understanding of not only the basic mechanics of a transaction and the client's industry or business, but also of corporate law issues, tax issues, business structuring issues, and other legal issues that are relevant to the transaction. The potential transaction's intangible factors, including personalities, leverages, and motivations, among others, must then be added to the analysis. All of this must be considered and analyzed in connection with a transaction.

Ultimately however, what may be the attorney's greatest deal making strength is the ability to clearly understand the client's objectives, always keeping the goals in focus and maintaining the attitude that the deal *will* cross the finish line. Unfortunately, in some transactions, attorneys do not appear to be motivated to see the deal reach a successful completion. Then, when those attorneys encounter a potential deal-breaking issue, instead of trying to craft a solution to the problem, they simply tell the client they have reached a deadlock or that the issue is a deal killer. Rather than adopting this pessimistic approach to deal making, however, the successful attorney recognizes that almost any problem in a transaction is solvable in the context of the entire transaction.

So how does the attorney maintain the proper attitude? The attorney should always keep in mind that when a buyer or seller agrees to pursue a transaction, he or she usually wants to complete the transaction. Although some people will just want to test the waters, most people who begin a transaction want to finish it. When a significant problem develops, rather than accepting the problem at face value, the attorney should understand that virtually every problem has a solution and can be managed through a number of different methods. Additionally, the attorney will often discover that instead of one issue, there may actually be multiple issues confronting that person. In these cases, to complete the deal, one party may concede on one issue in exchange for the other party's concession on another. This kind of give-and-take will often resolve the potential deal-breaking issues, and attorneys should be willing to work toward reaching a compromise when confronted with such problems. By working closely with a client, the attorney may find that an issue the client was stuck on is not significant or is tradable for some other point.

Egos, Emotions, and Education

The art of good deal making is the art of understanding not only the business issues present in a transaction, but also the parties' emotions and the leverage in the transaction, and being able to layer all of these factors together with the objective of reaching a common goal – completing the transaction in a manner that works for everyone involved.

This is of particular importance in transactions that involve private (non-public) companies. Many times, in connection with this type of transaction, the attorney is dealing with only one or two people who will control the deal, and in these circumstances, the egos and personal motivations of the parties can become much more of a force to contend with than when dealing with public companies. Regardless of the nature of the transaction parties or the number of individuals involved, to be an effective deal maker, the attorney has to be able to develop a rapport with and an understanding of all the people who are on the different sides of the transaction. To this end, one of the most important characteristics of being a deal maker, rather than a deal breaker, is not taking "no" for an answer, particularly when that answer is motivated by ego, emotion, or personal matters relevant to only one individual. In deal making, the attorney must realize he will run into perceived brick walls time and again. As a result, the attorney's attitude must be that there is no brick wall he cannot go under, over, or around.

In trying to push a deal across the finish line, first and foremost, the attorney must identify what is actually motivating his client, as well as the other party or parties to the transaction: Why has each party agreed to this transaction? At the most elementary level, the motivating factor is usually money. Occasionally, though, the attorney will discover other motivating factors, such as timing or, as mentioned, ego. For example, sometimes one or more of the parties, perhaps more often the seller, will agree to the transaction simply because the timing is right for that party, or for reasons personal to that seller – for instance, that he wants to complete a transaction with that particular buyer. Regardless of the motivating factors, having a good understanding of those particular factors helps the attorneys and the other business people involved overcome the problems and issues that surface during the course of the transaction. Additionally, the attorney must be able to identify the relative strength or weakness of each person's leverage with respect to a transaction. Only with a good understanding of the factors motivating the parties to a particular transaction and the leverage each of those parties brings to bear on that transaction may an attorney determine the most effective and efficient means to facilitate a successful completion of the deal.

Aside from determining his or her client's motivations and leverage, one of the most significant challenges for any transactional attorney is dealing with presidents, founders, entrepreneurs, and the like because of the personality factors that materialize when dealing with such individuals. Generally, these people are sellers who have successful companies and often are independently wealthy, a combination that often breeds an exaggerated ego. Usually, to bring such a person to the negotiating table, and ultimately across the finish line, the attorney must find a way to gain a measure of control with respect to that person and the accompanying ego issues.

Despite their business successes and indubitable intelligence, often these types of sellers have rarely been involved in this type of transaction and have no idea about the legal ramifications of a transaction. Such a seller may, for example, have no concept of what a representation or a warranty is, or that following the closing, he may be called upon to indemnify the other party for a breach of a representation, warranty, or covenant contained in the transaction documents. All he knows is that he is going to receive millions of dollars for his business, and he wants that money in his pocket as soon as possible. The attorney will have to be particularly diligent in educating this kind of seller and explaining, for instance, that he might have to return a part of the purchase price if there is an indemnification claim. To do this, it is imperative that the attorney discuss these issues and the mechanics of the transaction with the client from the very beginning of the process.

The client must realize that no matter how simple the transaction, there will be some difficulties that the client and the attorney will have to work through and some issues to which reasoned and educated decision-making must be applied before the transaction is actually closed. If the attorney has prepared the client with respect to these issues up front, then the process will certainly be much smoother.

Leverage: Gaining the Upper Hand

Unlike the art of understanding people, leverage is all about hard facts and clearly discernable circumstances. Ideally, the attorney will have a willing buyer and a willing seller with whom to work. Almost invariably, however, one party is going to be more willing than the other. Generally, the more willing and eager the party, the less leverage that party will have. Accordingly, recognizing the facts and circumstances that may make one party more willing than another goes a long way toward understanding who has more leverage in a particular deal.

The seller will have the upper hand in a number of situations. If the buyer is a public company that is acquiring businesses to grow and fortify itself, and the seller is a successful operating business that is well run with good records, then the seller may have the leverage. In addition, when industries are being rolled into the public market, it is typical for the seller to have greater leverage than the buyer. Leverage may also be driven by the number of buyers in comparison to the number of sellers. The more potential buyers there are, the more leverage the seller will generally have available. Conversely, the more sellers there are, the more leverage the buyer will often have available.

Buyers also have leverage in circumstances where no one else is buying, and the buyer has cash. If the seller has little or no cash flow, the buyer will again have the advantage. In such situations, the buyer can sometimes purchase companies for a fraction of what they may legitimately be worth.

An attorney should not keep this leverage analysis to himself. Discussing with a client each party's leverage is an effective way to inform the client about the process, control client expectations, and sometimes learn about aspects of leverage in the transaction the attorney may not have identified.

Leverage is having something someone else wants. In certain situations, leverage is nothing more than having cash. In others, leverage is having the right business in the right industry at the right time. Identifying those leverage points when they exist in a particular transaction, will always go a long way toward helping the attorney develop a strategy for a smooth and efficient completion of that transaction.

Winning at Negotiation

Certainly the central component of any transaction is the negotiation of its terms, and being an effective negotiator is a central component of any good transactional legal practice. Negotiations are as unique as the personalities of the parties involved: Each is characterized not only by the parties to the transaction, but also by the attorneys and other professionals involved in the negotiation and the unique issues of the transaction itself. A primary tenet of good negotiation is the ability to gauge the personalities of all those involved. For example, negotiations with a New York law firm will generally be completely different from those with a law firm in Wisconsin.

The first rule of negotiation for any attorney is simply to get along with everyone, and understanding personalities is the best tool for accomplishing this. While some people may be extremely intense negotiators, a good attorney can generally maintain a good rapport with anyone. Occasionally however, the attorney will encounter opposing counsel or others involved in the transaction who are outright hostile and belligerent. In those situations, the attorney will still have to deal with that behavior as best he can but, in any event, without engaging in similar behavior and also without letting that individual intimidate him or cause him to lose focus. Identifying these hostile and belligerent personalities early can help the attorney gauge his actions to pacify these parties before they have the opportunity to create undue tension.

Second, because negotiations often occur between counsel for the transaction parties, each attorney should keep his client informed with respect to the progress of the negotiations. Occasionally, however, negotiations between counsel may stall, and it may be necessary for the attorney to have his client become involved in the negotiations. At times the attorney may suggest a conference for the principals and the attorneys. In other instances it may even be appropriate for the principals and attorneys to meet to agree upon an agenda and identify the outstanding issues to get transactions back on track after they have become bogged down. Less often, when negotiations have become hostile, the attorney may suggest that the attorneys summarize the issues for the principals to work through among themselves. This last approach depends in part on how comfortable the attorney is with his or her client. If the attorney has confidence in his or her client, then this approach may be useful; if not, the attorney should avoid putting his or her client in a position where the negotiations occur directly with the other party. Under no circumstances should the client negotiate directly with opposing counsel.

The third rule of negotiation is to be persuasive without being offensive. The most effective persuasion is based on logic and reason and results from being able to analyze a situation and explain it well. The attorney should be able to give good and logical justification to support his position on an issue and should also be reasonable when considering the other person's position. However, it is also important to remember no one can win every argument. The attorney must be prepared to concede on issues of lesser importance, particularly where the risk to the client is low. Showing reasonableness in this manner becomes the basis of persuading opposing parties on those issues that are material to the attorney and his client, as well as earning the attorney the appreciation of opposing counsel.

Accordingly, throughout the negotiation process and particularly when dealing with hostile opposing counsel, it is advisable for the attorney to focus on the issues that are most important to his client and not waste much energy on less significant issues. Some attorneys believe it is imperative to make every issue a deal breaker. To prevail, these attorneys will spend whatever time is necessary on each comment, regardless of the level of importance. When confronted with an opposing counsel of this sort, the attorney should explain to his client that the attorney can either hash through the deal one painful comment at a time or simply accept a number of them without belaboring unimportant issues. Ultimately, if a position is taken with respect to a transaction issue the attorney and client cannot accept, and the attorney is unable to persuade the other party to concede on that issue, then the attorney and client must be willing to accept an intermediate position that will work for both parties, assuming, of course, that such a position may be reached.

If, despite his best attempts at reasonableness, the negotiations do not proceed smoothly, the attorney should take certain steps. First, as previously mentioned, the attorney must keep his client informed of the progress of the negotiations and his intended means of getting things back on track. Second, at the appropriate time, the attorney should consider having a candid conversation with opposing counsel, where posturing is set aside and the problems present in the deal are frankly discussed. Although this approach is not typical and depends entirely on the specific circumstances, it is often worthwhile. In addition, whether much headway may be made by having such a conversation may depend on whether the transaction is being impeded by a basic deal point or by nuances of the deal. For example, is the impediment simply semantics with respect to a representation or warranty, or is there a core tax problem or a core issue regarding the economics of the deal?

In rare circumstances, the impediment may be the attorneys themselves. If the attorneys are unable to work with each other for personal reasons, then they may either reach a resolution with regard to their personal issues or bring in another attorney to help with the transaction. Typically, though, if one attorney is having problems with opposing counsel, bringing in another attorney will not resolve the situation, and no measure of candid conversation between the attorneys will improve the relationship.

Fourth, good negotiators are patient and focused. Every transaction has its own flow and timing, which is a product of the parties, the circumstances, and intangible factors. Smart negotiators follow this flow and do not force reaching an agreement on significant or key issues before the time is right. Forcing agreement on an issue often causes a negotiator to compromise more than is necessary with respect to the issue. Also, regardless of the timing or the tenor of the negotiation, it is critical that the attorney remains focused on what is important to his or her client in the deal.

Most importantly however, when negotiating a deal, the attorney must approach transactions as someone who prides himself in completing "good" deals. Never just accept "no" as the final answer. Obviously, in some situations, "no" really does mean "no," but in many cases, it simply means "let's find another solution." If the attorney continues to work toward reaching an alternative position, rather than just backing away, in most cases, he will be able to turn the "no" into a solution both parties can live with.

To summarize, focus on the client's wants and needs above all else. Be persuasive but reasonable in your negotiations, and instead of taking no for an answer, be ready and willing to put forth alternative solutions to any issue that may arise. Be patient, and wait for the right time to reach agreement on key issues. Finally, always maintain your integrity with the client and with opposing counsel. If an attorney follows these "golden rules," he will be successful in his negotiations.

Doing Your Homework

When working through any transaction, the attorney must inform himself or herself of all of the issues relevant to the transaction.

To begin with, the attorney must have a reasonable understanding of the client's business (or the business the client proposes to acquire) and business structure and the legal and non-legal issues relevant to the business. This is crucial to address all of the matters that pertain specifically to a particular industry or business. Every industry and business has issues that are significant and important to it and that must be considered and addressed in a specific, rather than a generic, way. These issues must be identified, or the attorney's representation of the client will be less than satisfactory. Another important point is that an attorney must recognize issues that are not obvious. Sometimes the most important part of an agreement is what has been left out.

When dealing with a public company seller or buyer, the attorney should review previous transactions the company has consummated. This information is generally available on the SEC Web site. This will often give the attorney a roadmap of how previous transactions have worked. The attorney will want to review, among other things, the scope of the representations and warranties, indemnification baskets and caps, and the amount and kind of consideration paid in those prior transactions. In many instances, simply by reviewing this readily available information, the attorney will be able to determine whether the consideration his client is receiving for his business is within the range paid for similar businesses and whether the terms being put forth are reasonable in light of the nature of the transaction.

When dealing with private companies, on the other hand, the attorney should review general industry information. This can generally be accomplished by identifying a public company in the same industry and obtaining information on that company. At a minimum, the attorney should be familiar with what is happening in the industry in general. For example, if the attorney is representing a seller, it might be helpful to review purchase agreements used by a public company when acquiring businesses similar to that of his client. Such a review, at a minimum, will help set some basic parameters on value and other core issues to the transaction, as well as to identify specific industry issues.

Finally, the attorney must properly staff the transaction with other attorneys and support personnel. Staffing is based on both the size of the transaction and the speed with which the transaction must be accomplished. It is important for a number of reasons that the attorney neither over-staff nor under-staff the transaction. If the transaction is over-staffed, the client will wonder why so many different people are working on the transaction and may question the attorney's judgment and the amount of fees the client is charged. If the deal is under-staffed, the transaction will not proceed smoothly; the individuals working on the transaction will be overworked; and issues may be overlooked or not analyzed properly.

Evaluating and Communicating Risk

Risk analysis is important in almost every transaction. The parties will often become bogged down with areas that have very minimal risk but which nonetheless have become the absolute focal point of the deal – a perfect example of "missing the forest for the trees." Depending on the circumstances pertaining to the transaction, after the attorney resolves the most core issues, such as the deal economics and indemnification matters, the attorney may be well advised to avoid overdoing (devoting too much effort to) the minute details that have little or no consequence.

The attorney should, however, keep the client well advised of the effect of all issues involving risk that are present in a transaction, whether they are core issues or less significant matters, and work with the client to understand the risk analysis with respect to each issue and the actual likelihood of any liability materializing in connection with an issue. For example, what is the actual probability of a tax audit of a non-public company that generally is not subject to automatic audits by the IRS? In this scenario, the likelihood of an IRS audit may be less than 5 percent. Then, to take the analysis a step further, the attorney should ask what the likelihood is that the IRS will actually determine that there is a real problem. Again, this is a low percentage, often less than 50 percent, depending on the specific issue. When the attorney analyzes these percentages, it becomes obvious that the risk is fairly small and probably could be valued and priced, but in any event should not be allowed to become a deal breaker.

The attorney should also be aware that in some cases the client can obtain insurance on certain risks. For example, the insurance industry now sells products to insure against tax risks. If the parties cannot reach some sort of compromise with respect to any issue of potential liability, insurance may provide a solution. In almost all cases, when the parties properly evaluate the risks, they should be able to find a compromise within the transaction without resorting to insurance coverage for the various risks.

When to Walk Away

Unfortunately, despite his or her best efforts and a client's motivation to complete the transaction, the attorney will sometimes determine that what it will take to actually strike the deal is just not going to work or does not make economic sense. The attorney will occasionally encounter a situation where the two parties just completely disagree. For example, they disagree on the actual value of what they are buying and selling. At that point, there is very little the attorney can actually do. Unless the attorney can convince one party that he is either asking too much or paying too little or convince the parties to use an earnout to bridge the gap, it will be difficult to bring the parties together. In situations such as these, the best counsel the attorney can offer his client may be to cut his or her losses and terminate the transaction.

It is, of course, never the attorney's decision to walk away from a deal; this decision always remains with the client. In this regard, the attorney should always advise the client of any reservations he or she may have regarding the client's benefit in proceeding with the transaction. For example, in representing a buyer of a business, if the attorney becomes concerned about the credibility or honesty of the seller (or his counsel), it is imperative that the attorney advise the client about the situation. Similarly, in representing a seller in a transaction in which the consideration is something other than cash, it is incumbent upon the attorney to inform the seller of potential creditworthiness issues. If the attorney has concerns that the buyer may not be able to make the payments required under a note, and that unless the buyer obtains funding, its common stock will be worthless, the attorney should suggest to the seller that he or she insist on more cash up front and forego notes and equity as part of the consideration. If the seller is not willing to sell the business for the cash the buyer is paying at closing, the attorney must explain to the seller that there is a reasonable likelihood that the up-front cash is all the seller will ever receive. By informing the client of these concerns, the attorney has put the client in a position to determine whether to proceed with the transaction at all or whether more due diligence is necessary.

The Future of Deal Making

In the not too distant past, deal making was often simpler because individuals did not have easy access to information. Information is now more readily available to everyone and will continue to become so. This ever expanding access to information will continue to affect deal making by allowing all parties to be much more informed than they previously may have been. In addition, people (clients) continue to increase their sophistication, and, as a by-product, transactions continue to increase in their complexity. All of these factors have made deal making more difficult. The global economy will also have a great impact on deal making, resulting in more cross-border transactions and making transactions more complex by involving the laws and customs of different nations. On the other hand, the more things change, the more they remain the same. For those who understand (and can read) people and their motivations, understand leverage positions, stay focused on what's important to the client, handle negotiations adeptly, and maintain a proper attitude, the art of deal making continues as in the past. Clearly, to be an effective deal maker, one must not only work to perfect these skills, but must also endeavor always to stay ahead of his clients and colleagues on the information curve.

Kenneth K. Bezozo has extensive experience in representing business entities and individuals in corporate, business planning, and taxation matters, including structuring, formations, mergers and acquisitions, dispositions, and restructurings. He also has substantial experience in handling all types of federal and state tax controversies and bankruptcy and workout taxation.

Mr. Bezozo is a frequent speaker on business issues and taxation law topics, such as entity structuring and formation, acquiring, selling and restructuring business entities, federal tax issues affecting businesses and business planning, state tax planning for business entities, taxation of privately held businesses, and bankruptcy and workout-related tax issues.

THE ART OF NEGOTIATIONS

ROBERT CHEFITZ

APAX Partners

General Partner

Understanding Deal making

When I am called on to make a deal, I always try to have a good understanding of the industry the entrepreneur was in, which translates to an understanding of the challenges he was facing. Then I focus on that person's primary objective: Were they trying to build a big business or the best business? Were they interested in starting a public business? I try to really understand the business and the entrepreneur's objectives.

Sometimes this understanding is difficult to achieve. One of the biggest difficulties I face is poor communication. We will often come to the table with an intent that is mis-communicated. It comes across as a different intention with a different meaning. Often, someone may think we are trying to take their business away from them, and they will not understand how they are reacting, or over-reacting, to the situation because it is so remote from our true intentions. Poor communication is the most difficult hurdle to jump in the deal making field. Another hurdle is a close-minded negotiator, or someone coming to the table intent to get everything. That often becomes a situation you need to walk away from. It is necessary to test how reasonable this person wants to be and is capable of being. Having to do that once really sours the relationship through further negotiations.

One necessary element to successful deals is interpreting the true colors of the other side during negotiations. This will allow you to question whether the deal is sustainable, or whether they will perform under pressure – that is, whether it is even worth starting negotiations. The process of interpreting these true colors is extensive, yet mostly guess work. Going into a negotiation, you spend a lot of time in a relaxed environment, and the person provides references that, we hope, allow for true insight into their character. Deals come together very quickly now, as opposed to the first 15 years of my career, when you could literally spend four to six months, even nine months, getting to know the company, the individual, even their spouses, and having multiple occasions to spend time with them.

In today's environment, people just try to march a deal forward in lock step. The emphasis is usually placed on such factors as the source of funds or simply the execution of a deal document, when the real challenge is to spend time with the individual, which you have to do.

Additionally, when negotiating, certain warning signs appear. For example, sometimes people's behaviors are irrational in that their arguments center on emotional issues rather than business issues. Furthermore, you must analyze the position they bring to the table: Some come not as a partner, but as a real adversary. If they are adversarial, you have to be prepared to walk away. An adversarial mindset by either party in a negotiation will drag out negotiations, eventually making them tiresome and unproductive. There needs to be mutual respect and mutual trust for a deal to be made efficiently.

Nuances of Negotiating

If you must step away from a deal, the deal becomes harder to realize. Usually through negotiations, people can be brought back to their original premise. If they stay true to the essence of their business mission – that which made them attractive at the outset – then negotiating has a great chance of succeeding, despite the initial setback. If that does not occur, the discussion will struggle to move forward.

For instance, the party may be hung up on the issue of compensation. A counter-argument to this issue follows logically. For a company X size, compensation needs to be Y, according to size. If logical reasoning falls on deaf ears, then negotiation is not occurring in good faith.

If a deal progresses extremely slowly, a third party will be brought in to freshen negotiations. This third party needs be a good counselor, not just an attorney, and one who will understand the essence of the deal and hold both parties to task. Quite simply, he will encourage concessions from both sides. If the intervention of an attorney fails, the only remaining option is to turn to another partner. Introducing a new partner brings a rejuvenating freshness to the negotiations, and a unique, sometimes unseen, perspective that can help move a deal along. The bottom line is that a negotiator cannot be closed off to bringing a fresh face into the deal.

Negotiating is like chess. Great chess players know they are playing three or four moves ahead; so, too, with great negotiators. It is too easy to negotiate one move at a time and trap your interests in a corner. The focus must be on the end game, on the principles of the big picture, and on your purpose. A chess player plays to win, and the most effective strategy in fulfilling this purpose is to be four or five moves ahead, to avoid checkmate.

Once you know negotiating and the basic terms of the current negotiation, such as the business and the vision of the other party, the negotiation becomes second nature. You need to stay mentally flexible. I do not do a lot of preparation, or thinking about where I want a negotiation to go. An initial strategy planned in advance may prove effective, but sometimes one has to react to the flow of the negotiation as a chess player must adapt to the flow of the game.

This flexibility, however, must include seeing the big picture the deal presents. Successful negotiating breaks into two parts. First, I must convince the others of the big picture of the deal. Second, I must find a convincing and fair premise on which the deal is to succeed. It is easy to get people to agree to the big picture, but agreeing to the proposed premise is a little harder. It often occurs that a deal is two-thirds of the way to completion, when the company will return and say it loves the big picture, but the previously agreed upon premise suddenly seems incredibly lopsided. Then we must re-start the deal and negotiate a new premise.

The Mechanics of the Deal

The biggest difference between the two sides in a negotiation is that the venture business has a multiple portfolio, while the entrepreneur has a portfolio of one. Their portfolio contains one business that is their heart and soul. It is necessary to recognize and respect this. It is my goal that every entrepreneur I deal with feels that although tough during negotiations, I always respected both the entrepreneur and his or her vision. Young negotiators need to learn early that they deal with people's dreams that must be handled delicately.

When the deal is successfully completed, the balance of power shifts. Initially the other side needed our money, but after the deal is complete, we need their business to be incredibly successful. Venture companies hold more than

100 companies, too many to operate singly. There is neither the time nor the skill to do so. The day after the venture business writes the check, the deal turns into a marriage. It is a lot of hard work to make a marriage succeed. While buy-out agents are in a different position due to their control throughout the entire process, in the venture capital business, a transfer of power occurs that creates a co-dependence. Venture capitalists are a minority interest, meaning that several risks are adopted, 97 percent of the time.

Mitigating risk becomes an important step in successfully negotiating and acting out a deal. Gaining initial knowledge of a company and its goals is a simple way to reduce risk. Then several formal steps can be taken. First, the venture capitalist will explore other triggers that allow for changing the path to liquidity. Another is the question of whether it can gain control of the board to sell, if need be. Then there are up-front issues of management changes. Management risk often comes into play in situations where it might be the entrepreneur's first experience as a CEO.

Another formal step is to set up the reward to be commensurate with the risk involved, which could allow you to own more of the company, based on the massive amount of risk. Taking those steps may help you mitigate risk, but at the point that those steps are taken, capital is on the line at best, or at worst, money is being lost. Deals involving mitigations of risk make a negotiator feel successful, but it is the equivalent of cheap locker room talk because it will not help you to win the game because of the risk involved.

The game of deal making has undergone some changes that will continue. The time frame of deal making is changing. The pendulum seems to swing toward longer, more thought-out deals. We live in the day of 24-hour car loans and two-day mortgages, and some people expect successful deals to be made in 30 days or fewer – the faster, the better. However, there is now a trend for people to take more time in exploring options and individuals. This patience allows a venture firm to let the process unfold, which creates time to check developing quarterly numbers during the three months of negotiating. The pendulum's swing in this direction has created the trend that people are now willing to take their time, which makes for more successful deals through reducing deal risk by allowing the parties to make more informed choices.

The most dynamic and changing front in the field today is the relationship between large and small corporations to venture capital investors. There is a real challenge concerning the alignment of goals. For example, how do you take Johnson & Johnson's ambitions for a new product's development and venture capital's ambitions for maximizing returns and put them on the same page? This will take the most creative thinking in the field.

Personal Approach to Deal Making

I feel it is important to attain and maintain a strict business-like atmosphere during negotiations. I focus on the core economics. In the case of management options, I analyze what is available as a cushion, then determine that that cushion can never go above 4 percent. But within that cushion is some latitude around how the numbers are carved. I try to keep negotiations at a high level, focused on the business of economics. I let the lawyers handle the pressure of details outside the context of the negotiation.

In negotiations it is also important for the entrepreneur to know what the venture guy wants to do in terms of time horizons or investment size. Often venture investors are not explicit enough, which causes entrepreneurs to extract less than they need to run through the process. The process is detailed in the creation of investment memos, batting averages with certain committees, and knowing what is important to the committee. Often it is useful for management to oversee the presentation physically because of its understanding of the process. Knowing the process gives the venture capitalist an edge. For the entrepreneur to play ball, he must understand the game.

When sitting at the negotiation table, understanding, recognizing, and having advantages becomes a part of the negotiation. Most important to any negotiation, or even in business, is to have advantages in your mind and how they relate to the deal. Venture companies get presented with thousands of opportunities. If as a venture capitalist, you can keep that in the front of your mind – that you have an abundance of opportunities – then you will find you are in a winning position. Understanding this advantage allows you to ignore the pressure inherent to closing every deal. This is the biggest advantage venture capitalists have. We have a portfolio of hundreds of companies, while they have a portfolio of one. That in and of itself is an unfair advantage.

It may be unfair, but the nature of negotiation is holding onto an advantage, keeping it in your back pocket, and using it to your advantage.

Not every negotiation puts the venture capitalist at an advantage. Often we are minority investors. However, the best you can hope for in any negotiation is mutual respect, received and given, regardless of which side of the table has the advantages. After mutual respect, goal alignment becomes integral. Both sides must make sure that both interests are lined up well. For example, the entrepreneur needs to know the capital is good for a five- to six-year ride, but if he wants to leave his children a 20-year dynasty, the deal is misaligned. The two sides are not on the same page at that time, and they will continue their partnership in the future disjointed. A successful deal is balanced and aligned.

Negotiating Advice

The best piece of advice I ever received regarding negotiating was that it does not really matter. It is important to put the deal in the context of the bigger picture. It is easy to get lost in the mentality of win-or-lose. Just focus on the deal or the company at hand. This approach is reinforced in that you never know if you've won or lost for five to six years in our business. Sometimes a successful negotiation is one closed with no great "shake." Obviously, there is a lot of hoopla around closing and winning, but if that distracts you, sloppy business plans can sometimes sneak through the process undetected. Staying focused in negotiation means asking yourself if true goal alignment between the venture business and the entrepreneur has been achieved. If the goals are askew, yet you dance the dance for the sake of dancing, it will be a bad marriage, a long, hideous, horrible marriage – and divorce is expensive.

Honing your skills as a deal maker is a real mentoring process. You need to be very involved in deal negotiations. The venture business operates in a journeyman fashion. The lack of early stability makes succeeding in the field a process. The partner overseeing your early career will want you to be in every negotiation possible. First you will be a passenger, then a copilot; then you will fly solo. This process is important because it allows you to be there without the pressure of the negotiation, but as an observer, which prepares your negotiating skills well.

When negotiating as a team, the team has to work together smoothly. You cannot have someone running off as a cowboy negotiating something that is inconsistent with the deal as it stands. The team needs to be on the same page. If you have someone committing something out of line, you either have to defend the integrity and authority of that rogue team member, or you leave them out to dry and steer the negotiations back to the desired limits. If you contradict them as a senior negotiator, you ruin their effectiveness as a negotiator with that company.

Good individual deal makers need to be personable. They need to enjoy people's company. If they enjoy the company of the venture investor, they will be more willing to compromise, as opposed to compromising with a nasty and adversarial investor. Quite simply, you have to be someone people want to do business with. When there is an abundance of capital and an abundance of smart men with capital, the entrepreneur asks himself, Who do I want to be married to for five or six years?

Other important factors of negotiating include the ability to communicate well and efficiently. You need to be able to find out what is important to the other side; it may not be important to you, but it may be something you are willing to trade for. Similarly, the best thing an entrepreneur can do when negotiating with a venture capitalist is to give the appearance that although they really want to do a deal with you and are willing to execute and go forward, there are alternatives in the wings. In the absence of alternatives, negotiations can get distracted, and the situation can be taken advantage of. I think some entrepreneurs feel that the presence of another date would make them unfaithful. They reveal this attitude too quickly. They need to say, "I told you I am dating, and I will continue to date up until the point where I say, 'I do.'"

Robert Chefitz joined APAX Partners in 1987. He has more than 20 years of private equity investing experience. He began his career at Golder, Thoma & Cressey Co. in Chicago. He focuses on financing service companies in a broad spectrum of industries, with an emphasis on backing management teams to consolidate fragmented industries, including security, telecommunications, and information technology. His focus on services has led to investments such as Office Depot, Intermedia Communications, Protection One, and Xpedite.

Mr. Chefitz currently serves on the board of directors of CML Emergency Services, Inc., eMation, IntelliSec, Synchrony Communications, Inc, and VisAlign, LLC. He is a former president of the New York Venture Capital Forum.

Mr. Chefitz holds a BA in history from Northwestern University and an MBA from Columbia University.

VC FORUM

THE QUARTERLY JOURNAL Where Leaders INTERACT

Trying to stay a step ahead of the key issues every venture capital professional needs to be aware of? Interested in interacting with a community of senior venture capitalists, entrepreneurs and executives from the world's top firms? For only $195 a year, subscribe today to VC Forum, the quarterly journal for the senior most intelligence with respect to the venture capital business.

Sample VC Forum and Aspatore Published Authors Include:

Michael Moritz, Partner, Sequoia Capital
Heidi Roizen, Partner, Softbank
David J. Cowan, GP, Bessemer Venture Partners
Anthony Sun, Co-CEO & Managing General Partner, Venrock
Lawrence E. Mock, Jr., President & CEO, Mellon Ventures, Inc.
Terry McGuire, Co-Founder & Managing General Partner, Polaris
Graham Anderson, General Partner, EuclidSR Partners
Oliver D. Curme, General Partner, Battery Ventures
Jonathan Goldstein, Partner, TA Associates
Suzanne King, Partner, New Enterprise Associates
Mathias Schilling, Partner, Bertelsmann Ventures
Praveen Gupta, Partner, CDIB Ventures
Michael Carusi, GP, Advanced Technology Ventures
Mark Macenka, Testa Hurwitz & Thiebeault, Business Chair
Patrick Ennis, Arch Venture Partners, Partner
Gerard DiFiore, Reed Smith, Corporate Group Head
Sam Colella, Versant Ventures, Managing Director
Robert Chefitz, Apax Partners, General Partner
Daniel H. Bayly, Merrill Lynch, Chairman of Investment Banking
Eduardo Mestre, Salomon Smith Barney, Vice Chairman, Investment Banking

VC Forum is a quarterly journal that enables professionals connected to venture capital to cover all their knowledge bases and participate as a member of a community of leading executives. VC Forum is an interactive journal, the content of which is provided exclusively by its readership, and upon subscribing, new members become eligible to submit articles for possible publication in the journal. While other venture related resources focus on current events, specific industries, or funded deals, VC Forum helps professionals stay one step ahead of major venture related trends that are occurring 3 to 6 months from now.

With only 24 hours in a day, venture related professionals are expected to have a sound understanding of every aspect of the business, be aware of all major economic trends, and keep up with constant changes in the corporate world as a whole – a task that would be impossible without the appropriate resources. Each quarterly issue features articles on the core areas of which every venture related professional must be aware, in order to stay one step ahead - including trends in valuations, management teams, governance, exit strategies, M&A, tax and legal strategies, and more. Over the course of the year, VC Forum features the thinking of executives from over half the top 250 leading venture capital firms, investors in venture capital funds, investment bankers, entrepreneurs from VC funded companies, legal and accounting venture capital related specialists around the world.

To Order or For Customized Suggestions From an Aspatore Business Editor, Please Call 1-866-Aspatore (277-2867) Or Visit www.Aspatore.com